The Old Story of
SALVATION

SOPHIA LYON FAHS

Published

STARR KING PRESS

Distributed by

THE BEACON PRESS • BOSTON

Printed in U. S. A.

Library of Congress catalog card number 55–9360

Conrad

Library Copy

THE OLD STORY OF SALVATION

The Ark of Salvation

Life is like a voyage over a rough sea. The Christian church is like an ark; Christ and the cross, the mast and yard of the ship; St. Peter, the helmsman. The pelican atop the mast feeding her brood with the blood from her breast is a symbol of love. Above with the sun and moon are symbols of the four gospel writers: an angel for Matthew, a lion for Mark, an ox for Luke, and an eagle for John. The people waiting on the shore on the one side are friendly and on the other hostile.

Contents

Contents

List of Illustrations

Acknowledgements

Many yesterdays and many people have contributed to the writing of this book. Some have added to it unconsciously, to be sure, but my indebtedness to them is none the less for that.

It was a number of years ago, for example, that the boys and girls with whom I was working in the Church school of the Riverside Church of New York City sparked the idea in my mind. I caught it from the restless eagerness they showed to understand more about "our religion," as they put it, meaning the traditional religion called "the Christian faith." I am indebted also to my adult colleagues there who so willingly cooperated with me in experimenting with the re-telling of this Old Story of Salvation in its old and unexpurgated form. Also, Mrs. Grace Mayer-Oakes, director of the Church school in the Unitarian Church in New Haven, Connecticut, and two teachers in the Community Church in Germantown, Pennsylvania, faithfully tried out the story and submitted reports of their experimentation. The discussions quoted have come from the written records of these experimenters.

I am indebted also to the past and present members of the Curriculum Committee of what is now called the Council of Liberal Churches, for reading the earlier drafts of the manuscript and for giving their valued criticisms and encouragement. I wish to mention especially the three newly chosen part-time editors, Mrs. Edith F. Hunter, Mrs. Dorothy T. Spoerl, and Miss Lucile Lindberg, of the Council of Liberal Churches, Dr. C. Ivar Hellstrom, minister of the Riverside Church, New York City, and the Reverend Ernest W. Kuebler, director of the Division of Education. All of these have generously given me extraordinarily painstaking criticisms.

S. L. F.

Introduction

The Old Story of Salvation has often been called "The Greatest Story Ever Told." In whole or in part, literally or symbolically, it has been believed in by thousands and even millions of people the world around—and many people all over the world still believe in it. No other story has impressed itself so profoundly and for so many centuries on the feelings, thoughts, and habits of the people of Europe and America, as has this Old Story of Salvation. It has lived in the imagination of adults and children from generation to generation for nearly two thousand years. It has furnished the most important ideas for European art for centuries. English literature is saturated with references to its characters and its dramatic scenes.

Although it is quite generally assumed that everybody knows this Old Story of Salvation, few have ever heard it from beginning to end, or realize how much an acceptance of the full story involves. To many people it is like a piece of old and beautiful tapestry—they cherish it, but the key to its meaning has been lost to them. As a matter of fact, many would feel a little embarrassed if asked to explain the meanings of such expressions as "original sin," "the chosen people," the "elect," the "damned," "the Lamb of God," "the virgin birth," "the second coming," "heaven," "hell," and the "day of jugment." As long as such confusion prevails, there is the danger that what everybody is supposed to understand will become what nobody understands.

Our grandparents a hundred or even fifty years ago were not confused about its meaning. In general, they believed implicitly in this entire story. They knew what it meant, and its emotional impact was tremendous. In order simply to understand the history

of our Western world, and to know the inheritance our Puritan im-
migrants brought with them from across the Atlantic, it is necessary
to know this story. It was a powerful source of motivation for them.
It furnished the outline of their picture of the universe and of the
meaning and purpose of life. It was both their science and their
religion. It was the fountain from which they drew the water of
life. To fail to understand the meaning of this story in our history
is to deal superficially with symptoms without understanding the
causes.

There have been a number of different versions of the Old
Story of Salvation. It has purposely been told here in its oldest
form, so that it will be possible to compare the later revisions with
their original source. Biblical language and Biblical thought have
been preserved in large measure. This is the original "Christian
faith," presented in its great drama of human destiny. From this
original root both Roman Catholic and Protestant churches have
grown. This is the first edition, one might say, of Christianity, on
which revised editions of many kinds have been based.

All versions of this Old Story of Salvation, however, have much
in common. In all of them — even in the most modern versions,
which find myth and symbolism throughout the story — the main
character in the drama is God. Throughout the entire story God
speaks to men and they answer him. His thoughts and even his feelings and his long-time plans for all eternity are presented. As long
as the church fathers believed that the Bible gave them this one
unified story, and as long as they also believed that the Bible was
the word of God, then it had to follow that this whole story must
be true, and if true it must be the most important story ever told.
Although the different sects in the Christian church at different
times have deleted certain ideas from the story or given new
meanings to some of the old concepts, in its main outline this story
still retains a central place in all but the most liberal Christian
groups.

We have followed St. Augustine's pattern in *The Old Story of Salvation,* by dividing the events the book records into the Seven Great Ages of Time. In the fifth century after Christ, St. Augustine, like many of his contemporaries, regarded the number seven as the perfect number. Had not God spent seven days in the creation of the world and of man? Then why not expect that seven great ages of time would pass before the world would pass away? Only when the seventh great age was completed would it seem fitting for the drama to end and for eternity to begin. Seeing the Story of Salvation in this way also augments the dramatic feeling that the movement of events creates.

This Story of Salvation has often been called "The Story of the Bible," but this is a misnomer. Knowing this old story is not the same as being informed about the Judeo-Christian Bible. As the story is here told, it merely presents the old way of understanding the Bible. It is the way the early church fathers interpreted the history of the Hebrews, as presented in their sacred scriptures, and the books added to the Jewish Bible, portraying the life and teachings of Jesus and the development of the Christian Church. It is the way St. Augustine in the fifth century interpreted the Bible. It is what Milton and John Bunyan found in the Bible. It is the way thousands and even millions of orthodox Christians still understand the Bible history. But knowing this Old Story of Salvation is not the same as knowing the Bible.

In order to understand the Jewish-Christian Bible realistically, one must accept it as a collection of books all of whose authors were human like the rest of us, and wrote of things as they saw them. Biblical scholars recognize frankly that the sixty-six books of which the Bible is composed do not express a consistent point of view regarding either God or man. They realize also that ancient historical records, such as these, usually contain inaccuracies; that myth, legend, and historical fact are often presented without any distinction made between them. Scholars also point out that the entire collection is mainly about one ancient people and their great leaders and prophets, and that not infrequently the writers show a biased attitude toward other nations.

In short, from this more modern point of view, the Bible of the Christian church is not regarded as a unified book with one consistent "salvation story" in it portraying the history and destiny of all mankind. Nor is the Bible studied to learn about God and what he said and did. It is studied to find out how a certain great people thought and felt and believed about God. The book is studied, as any other history book or great literature is studied, in order that we may be blessed by an imaginative companionship with great personalities of the past, that our thoughts may be enlivened and enlarged. In going imaginatively into the past, however, we go not to find a pattern to follow or an authority to accept. We go rather to learn from man's mistakes as well as from his achievements. We go with open minds prepared to question and to criticize as well as to be inspired.

This modern way of dealing with the Bible is embodied in other books previously published in the New Beacon Series in Religious Education: *Moses* and *The Drama of Ancient Israel,* by Dr. John W. Flight; *Men of Prophetic Fire,* by Dr. Rolland E. Wolfe; and *Jesus: the Carpenter's Son,* by Sophia L. Fahs. We hope that an examination of *The Old Story of Salvation* will but whet the appetite for a more careful study of the religious history and literature of the Hebrew people.

This book, containing the Old Story of Salvation, is the old way of understanding the Bible. Even though many of us today regard it as a mistaken way, it is important for us to understand this old interpretation because it has for so long been the common way. This then is an introductory study of the great "Christian tradition" which is still living and moving in our cultural life.

We hope that readers will find the dramatic suspense of this old saga so engrossing that they will try to read it through from be-

ginning to end in a few sittings. One needs to see the whole pano-
rama to feel the full force of this great drama of human destiny.

In order to make this quick reading possible, the story has been
condensed. It actually begins in the first chapter of Genesis and
does not end until the last chapter of the Book of Revelation. This
means that in the Bible it covers sixty-six books and over a thousand pages. Few people have had the patience or the interest to
read the whole Bible through from cover to cover. Yet the Story
of Salvation cannot be truly grasped unless both the beginning and
the end are put together. In this presentation, I have tried on the
one hand to avoid a dry-as-dust outline of happenings; on the other
hand, it has seemed important to put enough concrete details into
the scenes chosen as steppingstones in the story to keep the drama
alive.

When once a reader or a group of readers have lived imaginatively through the entire story from the creation of the world to the
end of time and the beginning of eternity, it is hoped that the drama
will be re-read section by section and that questions and issues will
be raised frankly and discussed fully and fearlessly. Suggestions
will be found at the end of the book for those who wish help in such
further study.

The purpose of this small book is not to belittle the old tradition, or to hold up to derision the beliefs which still vitally motivate
the lives of millions today. Instead, this book represents a sincere
effort to do full justice to all the values there are in this Old Story
of Salvation. It is our hope that our readers will see in this dream of
human destiny more than a series of mistaken and outgrown beliefs beneath an intelligent person's appreciation. We hope that
the truths in it which have given this story such a lasting vitality
will be understood and appreciated. We hope that its intellectual
and moral shortcomings will also be examined and questioned and
understood so that what still seems true can be separated from what
now seems false. Without such a discriminating study, any liberal-

ism we profess will be shallow and short-lived. We must know the grounds for our own faith for the sake of our own mental and spiritual health. We must know also the foundations on which our neighbors have built up different faiths in order to be able to live with them with interest and affection.

This study is important, therefore, not that we may know how to combat orthodoxy, but in order that we may understand ourselves and others. If we are to contribute toward the development of a religious outlook more in harmony with today's understanding of our universe and of life, we must find a faith that will grip the interests and meet the anxieties of our generation as fully as did the "faith of our fathers" for the generations that have passed. To do this we must delve deep into life's problems, and we must touch with our own hands the roots of human despair and aspiration.

It may be a surprise to some readers to learn that other religious groups have believed in other divine saviors. Originally we had hoped to include two or possibly three other stories of salvation in this volume. After exploring some of these possibilities, we realized it was wise to be less ambitious. We have, therefore, contented ourselves with simply suggesting parallels to certain parts of the Christian story that are to be found in other scriptures. We hope, however, that this study of our own tradition will lure readers to a search on their own into books that present others of the world's saviors. Mohammed, as long ago as the seventh century A.D., said:

> Whatever be thy religion, associate with men who think
>   differently from thee.
> If thou art a Musselman, go stay with the Franks.
> If thou art a Christian, mix with the Jews.
> If thou can'st mix with them freely and art not angered
>   at hearing them, thou hast attained peace, and art
>   master of creation.

SOPHIA LYON FAHS

PART ONE

THE OLD STORY OF SALVATION

OR

THE SEVEN GREAT AGES OF TIME

Faith of our fathers, living still,
In spite of dungeon, fire and sword,
O how our hearts beat high with joy,
Whene'er we hear that glorious word!

— F. W. FABER

The First Great Age of Time

In the Beginning [1]

[Genesis 1:1-31; 2:1-25]

In the beginning of all beginnings was God, the almighty creator of all that is or ever shall be — the uncreated one — from everlasting to everlasting. Before there was any earth or sky, before there were sun, moon or stars, God lived in his heaven, a place of perfect beauty and light.

Underneath this heaven of light there spread endlessly in all directions a vast, watery waste of darkness, empty of all forms.

In the beginning — on an unknown day that was neither day nor night — the spirit of God moved like a breath over the face of the darkness. And God called, "Let there be light in the midst of the darkness!" And behold, beams of light shone down into the darkness. Then God separated the light from the dark. The light God called day and the darkness he called night. Thus God made the first evening and the first morning of time. And he was pleased, saying, "This is good."

Again God's voice sounded forth over the vast spaces. "Let part of the waters be lifted up above the rest of the waters by a strong arching dome!" So God created the dome of the sky, which

---

[1] The Bible references on which this telling of The Old Story of Salvation is based are given at the beginning of each section. Where the Bible language is followed, preference has been given to the new Revised Standard Version of 1953.

Certain theological ideas which are not found in the Bible text have been added to the narrative from time to time. These additions have been taken from the writings of the Christian fathers of the first few centuries after the death of Christ. The outline used, which molds the story into seven ages of time, has been taken from St. Augustine, who lived in the fifth century (354-430 A.D.)

we call the firmament, and he separated the waters above the dome of the sky from the waters below. Then there was the evening and morning of the second great day of time.

Once more God the creator spoke. "Let the waters under the firmament be gathered together into oceans and let dry land appear!" So the continents and the oceans of the earth were formed, and God called all that he had made good.

Then God said, "Let the earth put forth grass, and plants bearing seeds!" At once green growing things began to spread over the earth, and God, seeing them, said, "These too are good." And there was the evening and the morning of the third great day of time.

Again the creator spoke. "Let there be lights in the sky, to give light to the earth, and to divide the day from the night and to be as the signs of the seasons and years." So God created the two great lights—the sun, the greater light, to rule by day, and the moon, the lesser light, to rule by night. He created the stars also and placed them in the sky. These lights God called good also. And there was the evening and the morning of the fourth great day of time.

"Let the waters now swarm with living creatures, even with great sea monsters, and let birds fly through the open air!" When all these thousands of living creatures were born, according to God's word, he blessed them, and said, "Multiply your numbers by giving birth to new creatures like yourselves." And there was the evening and the morning of the fifth great day of time.

Then God said, "Let land animals be born—cattle, wild beasts of all kinds, and animals that creep on the ground."

Finally God said, "Let there be human beings, spiritual and immortal like myself. And let them rule over the earth and all other living things on it."

So God made a mist rise from the earth and cover it. Then he took a piece of moist clay and molded it into the shape of a man, and breathed into its nostrils until life came into the clay and the

God created the two great lights.

man became a living soul. God called this first man Adam. He placed him in a beautiful garden where there was every kind of tree that was pleasant to look at or that bore good fruit. In the center of the garden were two special trees—the tree of life, and the tree of the knowledge of good and evil. A river ran through the garden.

God said to Adam, "This garden is yours to tend. You may eat the fruit of any tree here except from the tree of life and from the tree of the knowledge of good and evil. Should you disobey me and eat the fruit of either of these trees, you will no longer be immortal, but will some day have to die."

For a while the first man, Adam, enjoyed the animals and gave names to them all, even all the birds and the wild beasts. But soon he became lonesome. He wanted a companion like himself.

Seeing how lonely Adam was, God made him fall asleep. While he slept God opened up his skin and took out one of his ribs, and from this God made a woman. When Adam awoke and saw this woman, he was pleased, and they lived together happily. In the warm and pleasant garden they went naked, but it seemed nothing to be ashamed of. And the man called his wife Eve—the first mother of all people.

Now when the earth and sky were finished, and all living creatures had been created, God looked down from heaven on everything he had created and said, "Behold, it is all very good!" And there was the evening and morning of the sixth great day of time.

On the seventh day God rested from the labor of creation, and he blessed this seventh day. He commanded that all men for all time should remember one day in seven to keep it holy, and that they too should rest on that day from their usual labors as God himself had rested from his.

The First Great Tragedy

[Genesis 3:1-24]

Now in God's heaven, one of the immortal angels had been strongly moved by an evil desire to rebel against God, and he stirred others of the angels to join him in his bold disobedience. So a war was begun in heaven.

But the Almighty quickly made an end of this by throwing all the rebels out of heaven and plunging them far, far down below the earth into a place of complete darkness called hell, where they were left to weep and gnash their teeth in bitterness. The leader of these wicked angels has been called the devil.

At last, seeing that the Almighty had created an earth and sky above, the devil flew up out of hell to look around on the earth. When he found the beautiful garden with its wondrous fruit-bearing trees, and when he saw the man Adam and the woman Eve living there together in such happiness, the devil envied them and determined to make trouble for them. Being still an immortal angel, he was able to change his form to suit his purposes. So the devil chose to change himself into a snake that could talk. As a snake, therefore, he climbed up into one of the branches of the tree of the knowledge of good and evil and waited his opportunity.

Presently Eve walked by looking up at the beautiful fruit. She longed to pick an apple and taste it. The devil, seeing her hesitate, said to her, "Has God said anything to you about not eating the fruit on this tree?"

"Yes," answered Eve. "We may eat the fruit of any of the trees except this one and the tree of life. If we eat the fruit of either of these trees, God has said we will no longer be immortal like the angels in heaven, but that some day we will have to die."

The devil scoffed at this. "God knows very well that you will not die if you eat the fruit of this tree. I tell you truly, if you eat of this fruit you will become wise like God, for you will then understand the difference between good and evil. You can then plan your life for yourself."

Eve looked up again at the lovely fruit hanging from the tree, so delightful to see. If it really would make her wise, why not taste it? So, trying to forget God's command, she picked an apple and tasted it. When Adam walked by to see what was going on, she gave him one of the apples to taste, too.

But scarcely had each one finished with his apple when a strange feeling came over them. They began to be afraid and ashamed—ashamed that they were standing there naked. Fearing God might come by, they began hurriedly to gather leaves and started to weave them together to make aprons to cover their loins.

But God in his heaven was watching them all the time, and he became very angry with the first man and woman. Flying quickly to the earth, he walked quietly in and out of the garden until the cool of the day. Adam and Eve were frightened when they heard footsteps, and tried to hide among the trees.

"Where are you, Adam?" called God.

"I heard some one walking about in our garden," said Adam, "and I was afraid and ashamed of being naked and tried to hide."

"Who told you that you were naked? Have you eaten the fruit from the tree in the center of the garden?"

"The woman you gave me asked me to take a taste, and I ate."

Turning sternly to Eve, God said, "What is this that you have done?"

Eve also tried to defend herself. "The snake there in the tree talked to me and teased me until I ate."

God then turned to the snake, knowing well that it was the devil in disguise. "Because you have done this, you are cursed above all the animals. You shall crawl on the ground and you shall eat dust all the days of your life. The woman you tempted shall be your enemy—she and her children and their children's children forever

Adam and Eve tried to hide among the trees.

and ever. They shall stamp on your head and curse you, but you shall have the power only to bruise their heels."

God turned then and spoke again to Eve. "Because you have done this, you shall suffer great pain when your children are born. You can no longer make your own decisions, for your husband shall rule over you and his desires shall be yours."

Finally God turned to Adam. "Since you listened to your wife, and ate the fruit that I had commanded you not to eat, I am cursing the earth because of you. It shall bring forth thorns and thistles, and you shall have to labor and sweat to make it yield enough food for you. And no longer are you and Eve immortal like myself. I created you from the dust, and in death you shall return to dust."

On that terrible day when Adam and Eve disobeyed God, the troubles of the world began. The human race experienced its first great tragedy. Fear, hard labor, pain, sickness, evil thoughts and deeds, sorrow and death came into the world. But worst of all, a kind of evil poison began to grow within these two people till it became a part of their very nature. Since they were the first father and mother of all the human race, every descendant of theirs to the end of time will inherit something of this evil nature. Every one will have to struggle between his yearning for love, goodness and truth on the one hand and his evil bodily passions for selfish enjoyment. So the first sinful act of disobedience was a tragedy not only for two people, but for all mankind till the end of time.

But Adam and Eve could not imagine the years and the centuries of years to come after them and the countless numbers of their descendants. Their own punishment was all that they could bear.

God himself drove them out of the beautiful garden into a barren country where they had to work hard, plant their own trees, and weed out thistles and thorns from growing grain.

Lest they might try to return to the beautiful garden, God assigned two angels to guard the entrance, each with a flaming sword in his hand.

The First Murder

[Genesis 4:1-26; 5:1-32; 6:1-6]

After a time, two sons were born to Adam and Eve. Cain, the older, became a farmer. The younger, Abel, was a shepherd. Since the two boys had inherited the evil nature of their parents, they often quarreled. Cain was jealous of his younger brother, because Abel thought himself superior. He called a farmer's work of plowing and planting less honorable than the work of a shepherd of sheep.

One day each of them decided to make a special prayer to God by offering him a gift from the results of their labors. Cain picked some sheaves of wheat and branches of berries and fruits and laid them out on a pile of stones before him as he prayed. Abel took a young lamb from his flock, killed and roasted it. As the smoke rose in the air, Abel felt his prayer rising up to God.

But all the while they were praying, Cain felt that God had no respect for his gifts of fruits and vegetables, and that only a lamb such as Abel's was acceptable. Cain was jealous of Abel's favor with God.

"Why are you angry, Cain?" asked God. "If you do well, will you not be accepted? And if you do not do well, sin is crouching at the door of your heart and you must master it." But Cain was deaf to God's warning.

Not long after this, the two brothers were alone together in a field. Cain was complaining. Everything seemed to be a sign that Abel was God's favorite. The name-calling grew harsh, their words turned into blows, and in the violence of his anger, Cain struck Abel and killed him.

When he realized that his brother was dead, Cain was frightened, and ran without knowing where he was going. But he could not run away from God. He heard a voice beside him. "Where is Abel, your brother?" asked God.

"I do not know. Am I my brother's keeper?"

"What have you done, Cain?" asked God. "The voice of your brother's blood is crying to me from the ground. The ground itself is cursing you because of the blood you have made it drink. It shall no longer give you back fruits and harvests of grain. You shall be a fugitive and a wanderer over the earth."

"My punishment is greater than I can bear, O God," cried Cain. "I have lost my home and my family and my fields, and who-ever finds me will kill me."

"No," said God. "I will not allow anyone to kill you. I am now putting a mark on your forehead, so that anyone who sees you will know that you have been cursed, because you killed your brother. Whoever kills you will be punished even seven times more severely than I am now punishing you."

On hearing these terrible words, Cain ran away and dwelt in a desert land. He was never to see his parents again.

Months and years passed by. Other children and grandchil-dren were born to Adam and Eve. As one by one the babies were born, so one by one the older people died, as God had said they would do.

But each new generation as it came was no better than the first parents. Indeed, they became more careless about obeying God's commands. They lived for their own pleasures, and the thoughts they hid in their hearts were hateful toward one another, and drunk-enness was common.

As God watched the growing wickedness of men on the earth, it grieved him exceedingly. He was sorry he had ever created the first man.

So the first Great Age of Time ended in deep disappointment for God and in tragedy for mankind.

The First Murder

The Second Great Age of Time

The World Flood

[Genesis 6:7-22; chap. 7-9]

God waited patiently many generations, hoping that men would repent and become sorry for their sins and turn to him to ask forgiveness. But the people of the earth were well satisfied with themselves. They took pleasure in doing evil, and their lives were filled with cruelties.

At last God said, "I will be patient no longer. I regret that I ever created human beings. I will wipe them off the face of the earth. I will destroy all the animals, too, and all reptiles that creep on the ground and all insects and all birds. I regret ever having made them."

There was one man and his family, however, whom God was unwilling to destroy. This was Noah, a good man whom God looked on with favor.

So God called Noah to him and said, "I am going to send a great flood that will drown all the people of the world, and living things of all kinds. But I will not destroy you and your wife and your three sons and their wives, if you will do as I say. Build an ark, three stories high and four hundred and fifty feet long and seventy-five feet wide, having a door and windows.

"When you have finished building this ark, go in with your sons and their wives, and take with you also two of every kind of living thing, large and small, bird and beast. When you are all inside, I will make it rain. For forty days and nights it will rain

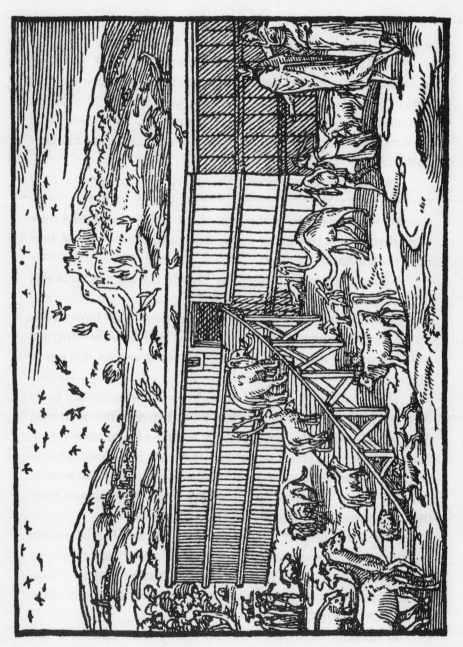

"Build an ark three stories high, and take with you two of every kind of living creature."

steadily until the whole earth is flooded with deep waters and until everything that lives and breathes is drowned."

After many years of labor, Noah completed the ark according to God's directions. He then gathered into one place two of every kind of living thing and led them into the ark. He took into the ark also large supplies of food to last for many days. When Noah and his sons and their wives were all safely inside, God shut the door of the ark.

Immediately the windows in the sky were opened, and for forty days and forty nights rain poured down until all the earth was deeply covered with water. Even the tops of the highest mountains were more than twenty feet under water; the ark was lifted up and rode upon the surface of the flood.

When at last every living thing outside the ark was drowned, God closed the windows in the sky and stopped the rain. Then day after day and week after week he made a strong wind blow to dry up the waters. It was not until five months later, however, that the waters were low enough so that the ark could rest on the top of Mount Ararat.

Then Noah let a dove out through a window in the ark to fly over the earth, but finding no place to set her feet, the dove soon flew back. Noah waited a week longer and then let the dove fly out the window again. This time the dove flew back in the evening with an olive leaf in her mouth. After another week, Noah let the dove out once more. This time she never flew back. Then Noah knew that plants were once more growing on the earth.

So he lifted up part of the roof of the ark and looked around over the drying ground. At last the fearful and trying months of confinement were over. Their day of freedom had come! Noah and his family and all the animals with them went forth out of the ark onto dry ground.

So thankful were Noah and his family to be still alive and free, that they built a large altar of stones. Choosing some of the animals they had rescued, Noah killed and roasted them as a thanksgiving offering to God.

Much pleased with Noah's offering, God blessed him. "From now on the animals are all yours. Be their master and rule over them. You and your descendants may not only use plants and fruits as food, but you may eat the flesh of animals also. But do not eat their blood.

"Build yourselves homes and have children. Let your numbers multiply. I make a promise. Never again will I destroy every living thing with a flood. As long as the earth remains, seedtime and harvest, cold and heat, summer and winter, day and night shall never cease.

"I am giving you a sign that I will keep my promise forever to you and to all the people of the earth. Look up at the sky. Behold a rainbow! Whenever you and your descendants for all time see a rainbow, you shall know that I will never again make a flood to destroy my creatures."

The High Tower of Babel

[Genesis 11:1-9]

As the years after the flood passed, Noah's family multiplied and became many. With each new generation, the children learned a few new ways. Some learned to be farmers, others became shepherds and cattlemen. Some made tools of stone and others molded plows and axes of iron. A few of the more original and artistic ones made music with pipes and simple harps.

All this time the people on the earth spoke the same language. They had found in the east a pleasant and fertile plain, and there they had settled close together and had started to build cities. They built their homes of stone, and some even learned to make bricks. But, alas, once more they became careless in their worship of God. As they learned more skills, they became proud.

"Let us make a big name for ourselves," they said. "Let us build a tower so high that its top will reach all the way to heaven." But as the tower grew in height, their pride also increased.

God came down from heaven to see the city and the tower which the sons of men were building. "Men are able to do these great things because they all speak one language," thought God. "This is only the beginning of what they will do. Soon nothing will be impossible for them. I will confuse them. I will make them unable to understand one another's speech. I will make each one talk a language different from his neighbor's."

Presently each man working on the tower discovered that no one understood him when he talked. As a result they were no longer able to work together and the tower was left unfinished.

God scattered the people far and wide over the earth. Each man with his family had to begin life over again alone in a place he had not known before. From that day on, the high tower men tried to build has been called the Tower of Babel, meaning the Tower of Confusion.

Thus God again punished mankind. This time it was because men were proud of themselves, imagining they could do anything — that they might even climb up into heaven and become as powerful as the angels or possibly even as God himself. This then is the reason why men now speak so many different languages, and why they are unable to live together in peace.

So the Second Great Age of Time ended. The children of men were confused and scattered and unable to understand one another and to work together. Again God, their creator, was greatly disappointed to find men so proud and ungrateful.

The Third Great Age of Time

God Chooses Abraham
[Genesis 11:27-32; 12:1-9; 15:1-6; 17:1-21; 18:9-15; 21:1-8]

In spite of many warnings and punishments, men continued to follow their own selfish desires. They even began to imagine there were many gods and they made idols of wood and stone and worshiped them, instead of giving reverence to the one true God, their creator.

Knowing how desperately wicked the hearts of men were, because of Adam's first sin (or wrong-doing), God slowly gave up the hope that all men would ever become humble and good unless he tried some new plan for helping them.

This was his plan. "I will choose out of all the people in the world the best man I can find anywhere, and he and his descendants shall be called my "chosen people." To them I will give my special guidance and teaching, and I will prosper them and make them a great nation. This people can then show the rest of mankind what is good and true. So by especially blessing and helping one people, I shall eventually help and bless all peoples."

God searched the world over for a good man after his own heart till he found Abraham, a shepherd chief and a Hebrew, living with his family in the city of Ur on the banks of the Euphrates River.

Appearing to Abraham in a vision, God said, "Leave this country where men worship false gods. Leave your father's house and go with your wife and nephew into a new land that I will

19

show you. I will make you and your descendants into a great nation, and they shall be a blessing to all peoples."

Obediently Abraham left his father's home, taking with him his wife, Sarah and his nephew, Lot, and all the sheep, cattle and slaves belonging to him, and set forth on a long pilgrimage to a land he had never seen. Northward and westward Abraham traveled. Whenever he stopped for a time to rest, he always built an altar of stones, and with the sacrifice of a sheep or a lamb he made a prayer of thanksgiving to God. Sometimes it was beside a bubbling spring, or under some large old tree, or on the top of a high mountain.

At last, after many months, Abraham reached the land that God intended to give him, the land of Canaan. He and his people were camping high up on a mountain. It was a dark night and the sky was studded with stars. A lamb had been sacrificed and eaten. Abraham was standing alone outside his tent door, when he heard God's familiar voice.

"Lift up your eyes, Abraham. Look northward and southward, eastward and westward, for all the land you can see I am giving you and your descendants after you forever.

"I am going to bless Sarah, your wife. She will bear you a son. She who is now childless shall become the mother of nations and of kings and peoples. Look up at the stars above you, Abraham. Can you number them all? In the years to come your descendants shall be as the stars — beyond all counting."

Then Abraham fell on his face and laughed. "Shall a child be born to him who is a hundred years old?" he asked himself. "And shall Sarah who is ninety bear a child?"

Inside the tent the wakeful Sarah overheard the conversation between Abraham and God, and she laughed too.

But God rebuked them. "Is anything too hard for God?" he said. "I promise you that after the proper number of months have gone by, Sarah shall have a son."

It happened as God had promised. Sarah gave birth to a son

The word of the Lord came to Abraham. "Your descendants shall be numberless as the stars."

and Abraham called his name Isaac, meaning Laughter. Sarah said, "Now I can really laugh. And everyone who hears will laugh with me."

When the baby was old enough to be weaned, they made a feast for him, and all the camp made merry.

Lot Makes His Choice

[Genesis 13:1-13]

Wherever Abraham journeyed, his nephew Lot went too, with his family and all his flocks and herds. As time passed, not only did the number of persons in Abraham's family increase, but the number of his sheep and cattle grew also, so that it became difficult to find enough good pasture land and enough water in any one place to supply their needs. Lot's herdsmen began quarreling with Abraham's herdsmen for the right to the wells they found.

Finally Abraham said to Lot, "Let there be no more quarreling between your herdsmen and mine. Is not the whole land of Canaan before us? Is it not ours? Let us separate. If you will choose the land on the left hand, I will go to the right. If you prefer the right hand, I will go to the left."

Lot lifted up his eyes and looked toward the east, and saw all the wide plain of the Jordan River. It was green and well watered, like a garden. But when he looked toward the west, he saw rocky mountains and forests.

Lot chose the plain. He moved as far east as the city of Sodom, beyond the Dead Sea, and settled there. But the people of Sodom were very wicked, doing only those things that gave them pleasure and forgetting to obey God. Lot and his family were gradually drawn into their wicked ways.

On the other hand, Abraham and his men moved their tents and traveled with their flocks into the hill country west of the Dead Sea, and settled for a while among the oaks on the hillside outside the old city of Hebron. There Abraham built an altar of stones where he often sacrificed one of his animals and prayed to God.

Three Angelic Strangers Visit Abraham

[Genesis 18:1-33]

One day during the heat of noontime, Abraham was sitting under the shade of his tent when he saw three strangers approaching. He ran to meet them and bowed low before them. "My lords, let a little water be brought to wash your feet, and rest yourselves under this tree while I bring food for you."

The strangers gladly accepted Abraham's courtesy. Abraham called to Sarah, "Bake some cakes quickly while I run and catch a calf."

Soon a servant was waiting upon the guests, with delicious calf's meat, boiled in milk, and served with hot cakes. Before his guests had been with him long, Abraham realized that they were no ordinary travelers. He felt they were messengers from God. Indeed, one of them seemed to be God himself.

When the guests had eaten, they rose and stood in silence for a while, looking off in the direction of the city of Sodom. Then God spoke. "I have been hearing many complaints in heaven about the people of Sodom. I am going over to see if they are really as wicked as I have been told they are. If the complaints are true, I have decided to destroy the city and all the people in it."

Abraham was frightened. "Will you burn the good people along with the bad?" he asked boldly. "Perhaps there are fifty good people in the city. Shall not the judge of all the earth do right?"

"If I find fifty good people in the city, I will spare the place for their sakes," God answered firmly.

"But, God, I have dared to speak once. I must speak again. Suppose there are only forty good people in the city. Will you destroy them with the bad?"

"I will spare the city for the sake of forty good people," said God.

"But," Abraham pleaded again, "perhaps there are only thirty or twenty or perhaps there are only ten good people in Sodom. Will you destroy them with the bad?"

"I will spare the city even if there are only ten good people in it," said God firmly.

Abraham was then relieved. "Surely there will be at least ten," he thought. The three strangers from heaven went on their way.

God Destroys the Wicked City of Sodom
[Genesis 19:1-30]

As evening was coming on, two of the three strangers reached the city of Sodom. Lot, sitting outside the gate of the city wall, saw the men coming and ran to meet them and bowed low before them.

"Now, my lords," he said, "turn aside, please, and spend the night in my humble house. In the morning you may go on your way." Lot urged the men so strongly that they went with him.

After they had eaten, the strangers spoke plainly to him. "God has sent us to destroy this city and all the people in it because of the many complaints that have been brought to heaven about the wickedness of the people here. But we will spare you and your family for Abraham's sake, if you will flee the place quickly."

Lot, terrified, went outside and told his daughters and their friends what the men had said, but they laughed him to scorn and refused to believe him.

Very early the next morning, as the sky was taking on that faint pink glow that slowly softens the darkness, the messengers awakened Lot and urged him, "Take your wife and your two daughters and run for your lives, or you will all be destroyed in the fire that is coming this morning on the city." But Lot was slow to act. Then the two men from heaven took hold of his hand and the hands of his two daughters and of his wife and forced them to leave.

When they were all outside the city gate, the messengers from heaven said, "Now run for your lives. Do not even look behind you. Do not linger anywhere along the way until you have reached the edge of the plain. Then hide somewhere on the mountainside."

By the time the sun had risen, before Lot and his wife and daughters had reached the mountain, God began raining fire and brimstone upon the city of Sodom and upon all the other cities of the plain. All the people there and every growing plant and animal were destroyed.

As Lot's wife was fleeing with her husband, she became curious to see what was happening. Forgetting the warning, she turned and looked back. Immediately she was turned into a pillar of salt. But Lot and his two daughters remembered and obeyed the warning of the messengers. They hurried on until they reached the foot of the mountain, and there they hid themselves in a cave until the awful fire had spent itself.

In the meantime Abraham had been wakeful and anxious all through the night. Rising early, he climbed the hill above his tent and looked eastward toward Sodom. He saw heavy clouds of smoke rising high in the air as far as he could see. The whole wide plain beyond the Jordan was like one huge burning furnace. Abraham felt sick at heart, but he tried to believe that the judge of all the earth had done right.

The Hardest Test of All

[Genesis 22:1-19]

Abraham's loyalty to God was to be tested again more severely than ever before. "Abraham! Abraham!" called the familiar voice.

"Here am I, Lord!" Abraham replied.

"Take your son, Isaac, whom you love, and go the three days' journey to Mount Moriah, and offer him there as a sacrifice."

Shocked, heartbroken, yet afraid not to obey, Abraham arose early the next morning, determined to do as God had commanded no matter what it cost. He awakened two of his servants and Isaac, his only son. He chopped the needed wood and saddled his donkey, and all four started off together toward the mountain. On the third morning, they could see it far off in the distance.

Later in the day, when near their journey's end, Abraham said to his two servants, "Stay here with the donkey, while the boy and I go on. We will make our sacrifice and then come back to you."

Abraham gave Isaac the wood to carry, while he himself carried the firebrand and the knife, and they both went on together.

Isaac was puzzled. "My father," he said, "you have the fire and I have the wood, but where is the lamb for the offering?"

"God will provide the lamb, my son," said Abraham bravely. They walked on together.

On reaching a fitting place on the mountain's top, they gathered stones and built an altar, and Abraham laid the wood upon it. Then he seized his own son and bound him with cords and laid him on the wood. He reached for the knife and was holding it up above his head, ready to strike, when he heard the familiar voice call, "Abraham! Abraham!"

"Here I am."

"Do not lay your hand upon the boy. Do not hurt him in any way. I have done this to test your obedience. Now I know you will do whatever I say, for you have not held back your son, your only son, from me."

Abraham dropped his knife and looked around. To his surprise he saw a ram caught by its horns in a nearby thicket. He immediately unbound Isaac. He pulled the ram out of the thicket and killed it as a sacrifice to God in place of his son.

"God did provide the lamb, my son," he said. "I shall always remember this mountain as the place where God provided."

Again Abraham heard the familiar voice. "Because you have

"Abraham! Do not lay your hand upon the boy."

done this, and have not withheld your only son, I give you my promise. Your descendants shall be in number as the stars in the sky or
as the numbers of grains of sand on the seashore. In blessing you
and yours, I shall bless all the peoples of the world."

Isaac's Twin Sons

[Genesis 25:19-34; 27:41-45]

Isaac grew to manhood, married, and had twin sons. The first
to come from his mother's womb was Esau, and the second they
named Jacob. Esau grew to be a skilled hunter, while Jacob became
a shepherd and one who worked about the tent with his mother.
Esau was his father's favorite, partly because the old man enjoyed
the venison Esau's hunting brought to the family table. But Mother
Rebekah loved Jacob more.

Esau, being the older of the two boys, was entitled to the family
possessions on his father's death. That is to say, the birthright belonged to Esau by law. If Esau had been a man who found favor
with God, he would have become the ancestor of God's "chosen
people." But Esau did not please God. He had married two women,
natives of the land of Canaan, who worshiped idols, and they had
led him into wrong-doing.

One day as Jacob was preparing a dish of lentil soup, Esau
came in from his hunt, feeling faint and hungry. "Please, Jacob,"
he said, "give me some of that lentil soup you are preparing, for I
am faint."

Jacob saw his chance to win an advantage over his brother.
"I will trade the soup for your birthright," he said sharply.

Esau hesitated. The birthright meant everything to him. "But,"
he thought to himself, "I am really at the point of death. What good
will the birthright do me if I die?"

"Promise me first that the birthright shall be mine," repeated
Jacob coldly, and waited. Finally Esau promised.

Jacob then gave him some bread and a bowl of lentil soup, and Esau ate and drank with relish. Then he rose and went on his way. Later, however, when he realized the seriousness of what he had done, he hated Jacob violently for having taken advantage of his weariness and hunger. "When my father is dead, I will kill Jacob for this." One day in his mother's presence he openly threatened to kill Jacob.

Rebekah, seeing the hate in Esau's eyes, became frightened. She secretly called Jacob to her and said, "Now, Jacob, obey me. Flee to your Uncle Laban's home in Haran, and stay there until your brother's anger turns away from you and he can forget the wrong you have done him."

As quickly as possible, Jacob got away without Esau's knowing where he had gone. To reach his Uncle Laban's home meant several weeks of lonely foot travel.

Jacob's Dream of a Ladder to Heaven

[Genesis 20:10-22]

At the close of the first day of his journey, as darkness was coming on, Jacob climbed part of the way up a rocky mountain to spend the night out under the stars. He found a ledge covered with many large stones; using one of the smaller ones as a pillow, he lay down to sleep.

While sleeping, he dreamed he saw a tall ladder standing up before him, so high that the top seemed to reach all the way to heaven. He dreamed he saw angels walking down the ladder and then up, and at the top he saw God himself standing. And he heard a voice. "I am the God of Abraham, and the God of Isaac, thy father. The land on which you are now lying I will give to you and to your children and your children's children forever. They shall spread their homes to the north and to the south, and in you and in your descendants all the families of the earth shall be blessed. I am with you, and I will take care of you wherever you go. I will not leave you until I have done all these things that I promise you."

Then Jacob woke from his dream. He was awed and afraid. "Surely God is in this place and I did not know it." He lifted the stone he had used for a pillow and set it up on end. Taking oil from a bottle hanging from his belt he poured it over the stone and made a promise to God. "O God, if you will be with me and protect me wherever I go, and will give me bread to eat and clothes to wear, and will bring me back to my father's house in peace, then you shall be my God and I will give you a tenth of all I ever gain."

From that time to this day, this place has been called Bethel, meaning the house of God.

Jacob pressed forward on his way to Haran, where he lived for forty long years. He married first Laban's older daughter, and later the younger. When finally he decided to return home, he brought with him a big family and many servants and large flocks of sheep and herds of cattle, for God had prospered him in all he had done. By that time his father Isaac and his mother Rebekah were both dead, and his brother Esau was ready to forget the old wrong. Later Jacob became the honored father of twelve sons.

Joseph Is Sold as a Slave
[Genesis 37:1-36]

Now Jacob loved his son Joseph more than any of his other children. Joseph's brothers noticed many small signs of favoritism. When Jacob had a bright coat of many colors made especially for Joseph, the brothers were so angry they could not speak peaceably to him. In his pride, Joseph began dreaming of being the greatest in the family, and he even told his brothers the dreams.

"We were all out in the field binding sheaves, and lo my sheaf stood up straight, while your sheaves gathered around it and bowed down to it."

"And so you are going to reign over us?" said the brothers in scorn, and they hated him all the more.

Joseph even told a second dream in which the sun, moon, and stars were all bowing down before him. Even his father rebuked him then.

The crisis came when the ten older sons were away from home tending their flocks far off in the hills near Shechem. Jacob had become anxious about them because of their long absence. He called Joseph to him. "Go now and see whether or not your brothers and their sheep are well, and bring back word to me about them."

Joseph set off alone in search of his brothers. As soon as they saw him coming toward them, they began to plot how they might kill him, or at least get rid of him.

Young Joseph was helpless against his ten strong older brothers. They seized him, pulled off his many-colored coat, and threw him into an empty well nearby. Then they sat down to eat their midday meal. Soon they spied a caravan of Midianite merchants approaching, riding on the backs of camels.

"Come, let us sell Joseph to these merchants!" said Judah. "Then we will not have to kill him ourselves—for after all, he is our brother."

It was quickly agreed. Joseph was lifted out of the well and offered to the merchants for twenty pieces of silver. The boy, with his hands tied, was dragged along after the caravan and was soon out of sight.

On reaching home, the brothers told their father that Joseph had been killed by some wild beast as he was traveling alone in search of them. Jacob in his anguish tore his clothes and wrapped himself in sackcloth, and sat mourning hours and days on end, weeping for his much-loved son. One by one the brothers tried to comfort their father, but he refused their comfort. "I will go down into my grave mourning for my son."

Joseph Rises to Greatness

[Genesis chap. 39, 40; 41:1-45]

In the meantime, the Midianite merchants arrived in Egypt. They re-sold Joseph to the captain of the guard of Pharaoh's household. Before long Joseph was made overseer of the captain's entire household. Unfortunately, the captain's wife became too fond of Joseph, and this made trouble; Joseph was put in jail. But even there God prospered him. He became the favorite prisoner. Soon all the other prisoners were put under his charge. They even told their dreams to him and Joseph explained what they meant, and in some cases he would tell them what was going to happen to them. Since his prophesies came true, Joseph's reputation grew.

Finally Pharaoh himself had some bad dreams. He asked his wise counselors at court to explain their meaning, but none could answer him. Then someone told him about Joseph. At once Pharaoh commanded that Joseph be brought to his court.

The Pharaoh told Joseph two very strange dreams. In one he had seen seven fat cows come up out of the Nile River and feed in the meadow. They were followed by seven other cows, bony and thin. And lo, the lean cows soon ate up all the fat cows! In another dream, Pharaoh saw seven ears of grain, full and large, growing on one stalk. Presently he saw seven other ears of grain, blasted by the hot east winds, on another stalk. And lo, the seven thin ears soon ate up all the large, full ears.

Joseph was sure of the meaning. "My Lord, O King, the two dreams are as one dream. God has spoken to Pharaoh through these dreams. He is saying that throughout all the land of Egypt there will be seven years of plenty, followed by seven years of famine. I advise you to appoint some man who is wise and set him over the land. Let him appoint officers to work with him, and during the seven years of plenty let him tax the people one-fifth of all the grain that grows, and store it away where it will keep until the years of famine come, so that the people will not die of hunger."

Because this advice seemed good to Pharaoh, he said to Joseph: "Since God has shown you how to understand my dreams, who is there so wise as you? I will now give you command of all our people. I alone will have greater power than you. Do as you have said."

The Seven Years of Famine

[Genesis 41:46-57; chap. 42-46; 47:1-26]

During the seven years of plentiful harvests, Joseph and his officers were busy gathering a fifth of all the crops and storing the grain away in granaries built in every city of the land. Then came the seven years of famine. The people began to cry out for food. "Go to Joseph," said Pharaoh. "Do whatever he tells you to do."

So Joseph opened up the storehouses and sold the people grain at a moderate price. The famine spread not only throughout all of Egypt, but also into the land of Canaan, where Jacob and his other sons found their food supplies running low. Hearing the rumor that in Egypt there was grain to sell, ten of these brothers appeared in Joseph's court, never dreaming that their young brother, whom they had sold to be a slave, was now next to the Pharaoh in power over Egypt.

Joseph recognized his brothers at once, but said nothing until they appeared a second time to buy grain. Then, when he told them who he was, his brothers were greatly frightened, for they expected him to take his revenge. But Joseph spoke kindly. "Do not be distressed with yourselves because of what you once did to me. I believe God planned that I should come down to Egypt before you so that I might save your lives. Go back home and bring our father with you. All of you must come and bring with you your wives and children and servants, your sheep and cattle. Settle here in Egypt until this famine is over. It is God who has made me lord of Egypt.

I will see that you never suffer from hunger." With these words, Joseph stepped down from his seat of honor, and went to each brother in turn and kissed him and wept on his neck.

So during all the following five years of famine, Jacob and his entire family lived in Egypt and had plenty of food for themselves and their herds, since God prospered them and gave them peace.

The Egyptians Turn Against the Hebrews
[Genesis 50:1-26; Exodus 1:11-22]

When the famine was over, Joseph's people no longer cared to go back to Canaan. Life in Egypt, in the province of Goshen where they had settled, had become very pleasant. Year after year they stayed on. The old father had long since died. Joseph and all his brothers were also gone—and all their children and grandchildren to the fourth and fifth generations—until there was no one left among the Hebrews who had ever lived outside of Egypt. Indeed, a Pharaoh was now ruling Egypt who knew nothing about Joseph. The Hebrews in Goshen were to him as all the other foreigners in his land. He said to his counselors, "There are too many of these foreigners in our country, and they are growing too rich. If we have a war they might join our enemies and take over the land. We must weaken them."

So Pharaoh forced the Hebrews in Goshen to work for him. He sent overseers to watch them and to discipline them. He forced them to make bricks and to build temples where his people could worship the gods. In spite of all his efforts, however, the Hebrews continued to increase in numbers. Finally, in desperation, Pharaoh commanded any one finding a Hebrew boy baby to throw him in the Nile River and let him drown. The mothers in Goshen were frantic with fear.

These were indeed distressing years for God's "chosen people." They cried to God to send them a deliverer to free them from their oppressors. But God turned a deaf ear to their prayers. His people had grown careless in their worship of him. They needed to suffer longer so that they might learn to live more humbly and obediently before him.

So the Third Great Age of Time ended. The Children of Abraham, Isaac and Jacob had fallen low—despised by their Egyptian masters, humiliated by their slavery, yet unable to break loose from their bondage. How long, O God, how long?

The Fourth Great Age of Time

A Savior Child Is Born

[Exodus 2:1-10; 12:40, 41]

The descendants of Abraham, Isaac and Jacob lived in slavery in Egypt for four hundred years and more. They groaned under their bondage and cried out to God for help, till at long last his plans for saving them began to unfold.

A mother among the Hebrews gave birth to a son. Fearful lest he be found by the Egyptian police and drowned, she kept him secretly in her home for three months. When she could no longer hide him, she made a basket boat and filled the cracks with pitch. She put her baby into the boat and carried him down to the Nile River, to the place where she knew Pharaoh's daughter came each day to bathe. She laid the boat on the water among the tall grasses by the shore, and told her older daughter Miriam to hide among the grasses to see what would happen. The mother returned to her home.

Presently the Princess with her maids came down to the river's bank. She spied the strange little basket boat and sent one of her maids to fetch it. When the Princess lifted the cover, there was the little baby crying. "This is some Hebrew's child," she said, and she felt pity for him.

Miriam listened breathlessly behind the grasses. She stepped out as if she had merely been passing by and had overheard the Princess's remark. "Shall I call a nurse for the child?" Miriam asked.

"Yes! Go and find me one," said the Princess. Miriam disappeared and returned shortly, bringing with her the child's own mother.

"Take this baby and nurse him for me and I will give you wages."

The overjoyed mother took her little son back to her own home, where she could now care for him without being afraid. When the child was old enough to be weaned, the Princess asked the mother to bring him to the palace. The Princess adopted him as her own son and named him Moses.

Through all the years of his boyhood, however, Moses' real mother never let him forget that he was a Hebrew. She taught him the Hebrew language, and told him the stories of his ancestors— Abraham, Isaac, Jacob and Joseph.

An Angry Moment and Its Consequences

[Exodus 2:11-22]

With the coming of manhood, Moses became more independent of his Egyptian instructors in the court. Now and again he would wander off alone and go to Goshen. As he listened and saw for himself with what strictness and even cruelty the Egyptian overseers treated their Hebrew slaves, he grew rebellious.

One day he saw an overlord mercilessly beat a helpless Hebrew, and Moses was so angry that he sprang upon the Egyptian and pummeled him to death. Since no one else seemed to be in sight, Moses hurriedly buried the dead body in the sand and went on his way. Word of the killing, however, soon reached Pharaoh. Immediately he called his servants and ordered that Moses be killed.

Moses speedily fled for his life, not stopping until he was entirely out of the land of Egypt and in the desert of Arabia. His one hope was to find some simple shepherd who would take him in and let him earn his bread by herding sheep. Finding a well where it was apparent animals were frequently brought, Moses sat down and waited. Presently a shepherdess came by to water her flock. Men also came with their flocks and rudely pushed the maid aside. Moses defended her against the men, and helped her get her sheep to the well to drink. As a reward he was invited to her home for the night. As it happened, her father was Jethro, the chief of the whole region. Later Moses married this daughter whom he had met at the well, and for forty years he lived with Jethro's family, sharing their tents and herding their sheep.

In the evenings as he sat with his father-in-law beside the camp-fire, Moses learned much from the stern wisdom of this out-door chieftain of many years' experience in the waste lands of Arabia, and he came to have a strong faith in the God who had created all things. The mountain whose cliffs rose high on the horizon wherever he wandered seemed a holy mountain — God's own special dwelling place.

The Burning Bush Speaks

[Exodus 3:1-22; 4:1-31]

One unforgettable afternoon, Moses was leading his sheep up toward the foot of this holy mountain. Before him he saw a thorn bush that looked as if it were afire. "I will turn aside," he said as he drew closer, "and see this great sight, why the bush is burning and yet is not burnt up." And lo, as he watched, he saw a shining figure rising out of the fire.

"Moses, Moses!" a voice called. "Do not come near. Take off your shoes, for the place where you stand is holy ground. I am the God of Abraham, of Isaac, and of Jacob." Moses covered his face, for he was afraid to look at God. The Lord had more to say.

"I have been watching my people in Egypt. I have heard their crying. I know how they are suffering. I have come to deliver them out of the power of the Egyptians. I will bring them back

A shining figure rose out of the burning bush. "Take off your shoes, for the place where you are standing is holy ground."

to the land of Canaan, the country I promised Abraham long ago. Come, Moses, return to Egypt, for all the men are now dead who once tried to kill you. Gather the leaders of the people together and tell them I have appeared to you and have promised that I will deliver them out of their troubles."

"But, God, who am I that I should go to the great Pharaoh of Egypt?" said Moses. "He will not believe me, nor even listen to me. I am not even a good speaker. Please, God, send some other person."

"Who has made man's mouth? Who makes him dumb, or deaf, or seeing, or blind? Is it not I, the Lord? Now, therefore, go, and I will be with your mouth and teach you what you shall say."

"O God," pleaded Moses, "please send someone else."

God was angry, yet he said, "There is your brother, Aaron. He speaks easily. He is even now on his way out into the desert looking for you. Let the two of you go together to the Pharaoh."

On his return home that night, Moses told Jethro all that God had said to him. He asked his father-in-law's permission to go back to Egypt. Jethro was very sympathetic, and said, "Go in peace!"

So Moses took his wife and his two sons and put them on asses, and together they set forth to return to Egypt. As he was journeying along, he met his brother Aaron coming out to find him. The two embraced and kissed each other and Moses told Aaron all the words that God had spoken.

When they were safely settled in Aaron's home, Moses and his brother called the leaders of Israel together and told them of God's plan to deliver his people from their slavery. The men believed the two brothers, and they all bowed their heads and worshiped the Lord.

Pharaoh's Stubbornness Is Punished

[Exodus chap. 5; 12:1-36]

Moses and Aaron continued to do as God had directed them. They went to the palace and pleaded with the pharaoh. "The Lord God of our people dwells on a mountain in the desert. Let us and all our people, we beg you, go three days' journey into the desert so that we may bring sacrifices to him and worship him."

But Pharaoh replied, "Who is this Lord God that I should listen to his commands and let your people go? I do not know this God, and what is more I will not let your people go."

Disheartened, Moses turned again to God. "O God," he cried, "why have you brought this calamity on our people? Why did you ever send me to them? You said you would deliver your people and now you have not done so at all."

"Be patient, Moses," said God. "You will see what I shall do for my people. Pharaoh shall be compelled because of his fear of my mighty power to let my people go. He shall even drive you out of the land.

"In the morning go back to Pharaoh. Meet him at the river just as he is about to go sailing. Tell him again that God commands that he let his people go. If Pharaoh refuses, take your rod and strike the waters of the river. They will at once be turned to blood."

Moses did as God directed. The Nile River became a river of blood, so that all the fishes died and the Egyptians could no longer drink the water. But Pharaoh's heart remained hard. He would not let the Hebrews go.

After seven days, Moses and Aaron went again to the palace. Since Pharaoh continued to be stubborn, God made frogs come up out of the mud of the river. They came by the tens of thousands. They hopped into people's houses, and even into their bedrooms and their ovens.

Pharaoh called Moses and Aaron back to his court. He promised he would let the people go if the frogs were gotten rid of. The next day God made all the frogs die. The Egyptians gathered the dead frogs in great heaps.

"Now let my people go!" pleaded Moses. But Pharaoh was firm. So Moses struck the ground with his rod, and at once swarms of flies flew out of the dust till the ground was black with them. They bit men and animals everywhere, except in Goshen where the people of Israel lived. There were no flies there. Still Pharaoh refused. His heart was hard as stone.

Then God made boils and blisters break out on the skins of animals and people. Many cattle and sheep died. But no one in Goshen got boils.

Since Pharaoh was still stubborn when this plague was past, God next sent a hailstorm. It ruined the flax and the barley everywhere in Egypt except in Goshen. In his distress Pharaoh called Moses and said, "I have sinned. I and my people are in the wrong. I will let you go. I do not want you in the land any longer."

So Moses stretched out his arms in prayer to the Lord, and the hail and the thunder stopped. Since Pharaoh quickly forgot his promise, God next caused an east wind to blow all day and all night. When morning came the air was filled with locusts. You could not see the ground because of the swarms of locusts on it. Before long nothing green was left on the trees and plants in all the land, except in Goshen where there were no locusts at all. For three days the swarms of locusts were so thick that the sky was dark and the people did not even rise out of their beds. But in Goshen it was light all the while.

Yet when God sent a west wind to blow the swarms of locusts away, Pharaoh's heart was again hardened, and he refused to let the people of Israel go.

Finally the most terrible of all the plagues came. God threatened to kill the first-born son in every family in the land, from

Pharaoh's household to that of the maidservant who ground the grain. God would kill also the first-born of all the cattle and sheep. But in the land of Goshen no one would die, provided every family in Israel followed God's instructions.

"Let each family among you select from his flock a lamb for roasting," said God. "When you kill it save the blood in a basin. On the evening of the fourteenth day of this month, let the head man of each household take a bunch of hyssop and dip it in the blood in the basin. Then let him sprinkle this blood on the lintel above the door of his house, and on the doorposts on both sides. Every one of you must stay indoors all night. Roast your lambs and serve them with bitter herbs and unleavened bread. Eat hurriedly so that you will have time to prepare yourselves for a long journey. In the early morning, be ready to go forth out of your houses and away."

It all happened as God had planned. At midnight an angel flew from house to house over the whole land of Egypt. Whenever he passed by a door on which were no blotches of blood, the angel slew the first-born son in the house. Not an Egyptian home escaped, from the palace of Pharaoh to the cabin where the father was away in prison. Loud and heart-breaking crying rose from every house in the land — except from the homes in Goshen. There every home was passed by. Not even a dog growled during the night.

In anger and fright, Pharaoh rose in the middle of the night and called for Moses and Aaron. "Take your flocks and your herds, as you have been asking to do, and be gone! I never want to see your faces again."

The Hebrews Flee From Their Egyptian Oppressors
[Exodus 12:14-20; 33-51]

Early in the morning the people of Israel hurried off, taking with them their pots and their bowls and what food they could carry. They gathered their sheep and cattle, and before the sun was up they were on their way.

Four hundred and thirty years before when Jacob and his sons and their families had come down into Egypt to escape famine, there were but seventy persons in all. Now there were six hundred thousand able-bodied men among them who could trek on foot through any desert, and thousands of old men, women and children besides who had to be carried on asses' backs.

And God went with his people. During the daytime he went before them in a cloud to show them the way. In the darkness, he led them by means of a pillar of fire.

Their great day of deliverance was the fifteenth day of the month of Abib. It was a day never to be forgotten by the people of Israel. It has been called the Day of the Passover because on that night the angel of God "passed over" the homes of Israel without doing them harm, while at the same time he punished the families of their Egyptian oppressors. On this great day God renewed his promise to lead his "chosen people" back to the land of Canaan and to make them a great nation and a blessing to all mankind.

The Winds and the Seas Obey God's Word
[Exodus 14:5-31; 15:1-21]

The next morning, when Pharaoh was told that all the Hebrews had fled, he became alarmed. "What is this that we have done, that we have let Israel go from serving us?" he asked. Quickly he summoned six hundred charioteers and a large army, and they hurried in pursuit. The Hebrews had just reached the shores of the Red Sea when the Egyptian army found them.

When watchmen at the rear of the Hebrew caravan reported that an Egyptian army was close behind, the people of Israel were frightened. They cried out to Moses, "Is it because there are no graves in Egypt that you have taken us away to die in the desert? Is not this what we said to you often: 'Let us alone and let us serve the Egyptians'? For it would have been better to serve the Egyptians than to die here."

"Don't be afraid!" said Moses. "Stand firm! God will save you." Then the cloud that went before them, moved behind them so that there was darkness between them and the Egyptians.

Moses stretched forth his rod over the waters of the Red Sea, as God directed. A strong east wind began blowing. Presently the waters divided, and there was dry land between two high walls of water. Promptly the hosts of Israel stepped down into the bed of the sea and walked safely across to the other shore.

With the coming of daylight, the Egyptians saw the dry passageway through the sea. So they drove down onto the ocean bed and tried to cross also. But God, watching from his cloud above, made their chariots sink into the mud, till their wheels broke off as the horses tried in vain to pull them out.

God again commanded Moses to stretch out his rod over the sea. This time the waters that had stood as two walls on either side of the path rushed back into their usual bed till all the Egyptians and their horses and their chariots were covered. Not one of them escaped alive.

When the people of Israel saw this marvelous act that God had done, they were convinced that Moses was his true servant. Miriam, Moses' sister, wild with excitement, called all the women to join in a dance of thanksgiving. Taking their tambourines in their hands, they danced and leaped and shouted and sang.

Sing unto the Lord, for he has triumphed gloriously:

The horse and his rider he has thrown into the sea.

Bread And Meat From Heaven
[Exodus 16:1-36; 17:1-7; Numbers 11:1-35]

When all was again quiet, the people of Israel began to feel safe. They gathered up their tents and started once more on their journey toward the land of Canaan. But much of the desert through which they had to pass was waterless and barren. Plants for food and animals for meat were hard to find, and the time came when the supplies of food they had brought with them were exhausted. Again the people began complaining.

"Would that we had died in Egypt where we could sit beside pots of boiling meat, and where we had bread enough to fill us. Now you have brought us into this desert only to starve us to death."

But God was prepared to save his people. "Don't be afraid!" he said. "I will rain bread down from heaven upon this land."

Behold, in the morning the wonder appeared! When the dew was melted, the people saw white flakes, a little like frost and a little like handfuls of small seeds, scattered all over the ground. They gathered this heavenly bread, ground it, mixed it with water and baked it. It tasted like wafers sweetened with honey, and they called it *manna*.

"Gather only as much as you will need for one day," said Moses, "for God will send us a fresh supply each morning. But on the sixth day of the week gather a double portion, for none will fall on the Sabbath." So the people were fed day by day with *manna* from heaven.

But as the weeks passed, some became dissatisfied. Eating the same diet—even a diet of *manna*—day after day without any change began to be tiresome, and the people again complained. "O that we had meat to eat!" they cried. "We remember the fish we used to have in Egypt without its costing us a penny, and the

Behold in the morning they gathered the heavenly bread.

cucumbers, the leeks, the melons, the onions and the garlic! But now there is nothing at all but this *manna* to eat."

Moses heard his people groaning all over the camp, each man at his own tent door. "O God," he cried, "why have I not found favor with you? How am I to get meat to give to all this people? Where is that land you promised our ancestors to give us? If I must continue to listen to their complaining, kill me, O God, kill me. I cannot bear this burden alone."

God answered, "Tell the people that even today at twilight they shall have meat to eat."

Near dusk that evening a strong wind blew in from the sea and with it came thousands of quails. They dropped as if exhausted and lay scattered all around the camp for the distance of a day's journey. The people of Israel excitedly ran out and gathered the quails in baskets—more than they could eat in one day. A few tried to keep them for a second day's use, but God was angry with them for not obeying his instructions. By the next day the leftover meats had spoiled, and those who ate them became sick. Some even died. From this experience the people learned to trust God to provide.

At another time, they were camped where there was no water. Again the people complained, and Moses appealed to God. "What shall I do now, O God? The people are almost ready to kill me."

"Take your rod, Moses, and go out to the great rock on the edge of the valley. Strike the rock and I will make water gush out and my people shall have all the water they need."

Moses followed God's directions. Water gushed out of the rock in a strong stream and everyone in the camp had all he wanted to drink. Even all the sheep and oxen were satisfied as well.

God Speaks From Mount Sinai

[Exodus chap. 19, 20; 24:1-18]

After another month of journeying, the people of Israel reached the valley at the foot of the holy mountain of Sinai. They camped in its awesome shadow. The cloud that hung over its peak seemed to hide a fearful mystery. The rumbling thunder and the flashing lightning frightened them. Moses commanded the people to bathe and to wash their clothes in order to be worthy to stand before God.

On the third day after this, Moses led the people out of the camp and they all gathered at the foot of the holy mountain. A black cloud covered its peak. Moses warned the people against going any nearer the mountain, lest they die. He alone could hear God speaking: "Go, cut two rock slabs out of the mountain, and in the morning climb to the top, for I will speak with you there alone."

Moses cut out two stone tablets and in the morning he climbed alone to the top. There he talked with God. And there God himself etched on the two stone tablets the ten most important commandments for his people. God also explained many other matters to Moses, for Moses stayed on the mountain top alone with God for forty days and forty nights.

All the while that Moses was away from his people, a thick cloud covered the mountain's peak. Whenever the thunder roared or the lightning flashed, the people said, "God is speaking," and they were afraid. As they waited day after day and week after week, and Moses did not return, they began to fear that he was no longer alive.

A Calf Is Molded and Worshiped
[Exodus 32:1-29]

Finally they went to Moses' brother, Aaron, and said, "We do not know what has become of our leader. Perhaps God has killed him. Perhaps God is angry with us and is not willing to be our God any longer. Come, Aaron, make us another god — one that we can see, who will go before us and lead us into Canaan."

Since Aaron also had almost lost hope of his brother's return, he yielded to the people's pleading. "Let your wives and your sons and daughters take the gold rings off their ears and the gold bracelets off their arms and let them bring them all to me. I will make you a new god."

So all the people brought their gold rings and bracelets to Aaron. He took all this gold and melted it over a fire. Certain men skilled in sculpturing molded the gold into the shape of a calf. When it was finished, Aaron set the image on a pedestal, and said to the people, "Here now is your god. This is he who brought us out of the land of Egypt and who will be our guardian god as we go forward."

Aaron made a proclamation for all to hear. "Tomorrow we shall hold a festival in honor of our new god." So the people gathered early the next day. An ox was roasted on an altar before the golden calf, while the people danced and sang their songs of praise.

But, high on the mountain top, God could see all that was happening in the valley below. "Arise, Moses!" he said. "Go down quickly to your people, for they have already turned aside from the way I have commanded them and they have made an idol and are worshiping it."

Moses hurried down the mountain, carrying in his arms the two tablets of stone on which God had etched his ten commandments. As soon as Moses came near the camp and saw the golden calf and the people dancing around it, his anger burned hot. He threw the two tablets of stone against a rock and broke them in pieces. Walking over to the pedestal on which the golden calf stood, he knocked the idol down and ordered that the gold of which it had been made be ground into powder and scattered in the brook that flowed near the camp. When this was done, Moses required the people to drink the water in the brook as a punishment for their great sin.

God Forgives and Makes A New Covenant
[Exodus 32:30-35; chap. 34-40]

This whole agonizing experience was so terribly disappointing to Moses that he felt he must once more climb the mountain and beg God to forgive his people. He cut two more tablets of stone from the mountain rock, and early one morning with a heavy heart he once more began the steep climb up the mountain.

When at last he found God at the top, Moses bowed low before him. "O God!" he cried. "This people have done a great sin. They have made themselves a god of gold. Yet now, if you will once more forgive their sin. . . ." Moses hesitated. He was afraid to say the words that he wanted to say. "If not, I beg you, blot me out of your book of life."

But God said, "The one who sins, his is the name I will blot out of my book of life—but not yours, Moses."

God then took the two tablets of stone from Moses, and again he etched on them the ten commandments. "Take these," said God. "Go back to my people. Tell them I forgive, and I will still lead them forward into the land of Canaan."

With this encouraging assurance, Moses returned down the mountain carrying the two new tablets of stone. He did not know that his face was shining with a radiance such as the people had never before seen. "He has been talking with God," they said in whispers.

It took many days for Moses to tell all the things God had said to him on the mountain, for God had given him very detailed plans for the journey ahead. He described the kind of ark or wooden box Moses was to have made in which the two tablets of stone could always be kept. It was to be carried on poles, slung over the shoulders of four men wherever the people of Israel went. A special tent, called a tabernacle, was to be built in which the ark could be housed. This tent also was to go with God's people wherever they went. God himself would hover over it in a cloud to remind them he was near. Whenever Moses was troubled he was to go into this tabernacle and stand before the ark and ask God the questions that were troubling him, and God would give him the answers.

Under Moses' guidance, the people made both the ark and the tabernacle as God had planned. From then on, whenever Moses went into the tabernacle, the cloud would drop low and hang before the door, and God and Moses would talk together in the dark of the tent. The people came to feel that Moses talked with God like a friend, face to face.

When all these things had been done, the people of Israel pulled up their tent posts and moved along toward their goal — the land of Canaan. The ark went always before them leading the way, with God hovering above in a cloud during the day and in a pillar of light by night.

The Report of the Spies and What Came of It
[Numbers 13; 14:1-38]

At last the people of Israel neared the southern edge of Canaan, and they began to wonder what this "promised land" was really like and what sort of people already lived there.

God said to Moses, "Choose twelve leading men, one from each tribe. Send them ahead into Canaan as spies."

Moses therefore chose twelve men, one from each tribe, and said to them, "Go up ahead of us into this 'promised land.' Find out if it is fertile or barren, if the people are strong or weak, rich or poor, few or many. Find out how well their cities are fortified, and bring back samples of their fruits."

The people waited in camp for forty days before the spies returned. What a surprise was in store for them! Two of the twelve came carrying between them one large bunch of grapes hung on a pole across their shoulders. The others brought samples of figs and pomegranates.

"The land to which you sent us," they said, "is very fertile. You might say it is flowing with milk and honey. You can see for yourselves the kinds of fruit that grow there. But the people of Canaan are strong. They all semed like giants to us, and we felt like grasshoppers beside them. They live in large walled cities that are strongly fortified. We simply are not able to go into their land and conquer them."

The people of Israel raised a loud cry on hearing this report. They wept all night long. "Would that we had died in Egypt. Or would that we had died in this desert. Why does God bring us into this land only to let us fall by the sword? Our wives and our children will be made captives. Let us even now choose a new captain and go back to Egypt."

But two of the spies, Joshua and Caleb, were distressed to see the people weeping. They had a different report to give. They said, "It is true that the land we visited is a very fertile land. And the people are strong, and their cities are well fortified. But if God continues to delight in us, he will help us. Have you forgotten the many wonders he has already done for us? Be strong and of good courage. God will give us this land which he promised to our fathers."

Then the cloud dropped down in front of the holy tabernacle. God was calling Moses. "How long will this people despise me? How long will they not believe in me in spite of all the wonders I have done? I will punish them now for their cowardice by sending a contagious disease to spread among them. I reject them. No longer will they be my 'chosen people.'"

But Moses pleaded with God. "If you do this, O God, what will the Egyptians say when they hear of it? If you kill this people, then the nations of the world will say, 'The God of the Israelites was not a strong enough God. He could not keep his promise.' You have been merciful, O God, many times before. Forgive this people still another time."

If Moses could forgive, surely God could too. He said, "I will yield to your pleading, Moses. This people shall in time enter Canaan and conquer it, but none of these men and women who have been complaining shall see the land — except Joshua and Caleb. Tell these people that what they have been wishing for will come true. They shall remain in this desert land where they will die. They shall continue to keep sheep here for forty years until all who are now twenty years old and more are dead. Only their children will I allow to enter the land of Canaan and conquer it. And by that time, you, Moses, will be too old to be their captain. I will appoint Joshua to take your place and he shall lead them into this 'promised land.'"

Forty Years of Wandering in the Desert

[Deuteronomy 6:10-15; 30:15-20; 31:1-8]

So it happened just as God had said. The people of Israel wandered for forty long years from oasis to oasis in the desert, tending their flocks. One by one the older ones died. As long as Moses lived he was their law-giver and judge. He spent long hours writing down the laws that God gave him to guide his people after they reached Canaan. These were all carefully kept on scrolls in the ark in the tabernacle. Of all the things that he commanded the people, there were two things which he especially emphasized.

"When you come to live in great and splendid cities which you did not build, when you live in houses full of all kinds of comforts with which you did not fill them, when you draw water from cisterns you did not hew out, and you gather fruit from vineyards and olive groves you did not plant, then take care that you do not forget the God who brought you out of slavery in Egypt. Stand in awe before him, and worship him only. When you find the inhabitants of the land bowing down before images of gods you have not heard of, do not copy them, but rather tear down their altars and burn up their idols. Bring your offerings and your prayers to the Lord God only. Do not make any treaties with the people of the land. Do not show them any mercy. Do not let your sons marry their daughters. Destroy them completely, so that you will not be tempted to be like them.

"If you will remember these instructions, God will bless you in all your undertakings, but if you forget these commands and do not observe them, God will send troubles upon you even greater than he sent on the Egyptians. Behold, I put before you life and good, or death and evil. Therefore, choose life so that you as well as your descendants may live in the land which the Lord God promised your fathers."

The Death of Moses

[Deuteronomy 34:1-12]

When Moses reached the age of one hundred and twenty years, God said to him, "The time for you to die is drawing near. Climb Mount Nebo. From its top you will be able to look out over the land that I shall give my people."

So Moses climbed Mount Nebo, and from its height God

showed him all the land of Canaan from the Jordan Valley to the great Mediterranean Sea—north and south, east and west. "This is the land which I promised to Abraham, Isaac, and Jacob. Although you yourself will not go over the Jordan into the promised land, yet will I give it to your descendants."

Soon afterwards, Moses died on the mountain, and his body was buried in a ravine where no one could mark the place.

For many years afterwards it was often said, "There has never been a prophet like Moses, whom God knew face to face, nor has there been one through whom God did so many great and mighty wonders."

So the Fourth Great Age of Time came to an end. None of those who had fled from Egypt had reached the "promised land." Even their deliverer himself was dead. Without him, would their descendants be able to conquer Canaan?

The Fifth Great Age of Time

Joshua Leads His People Into The Promised Land

[Joshua chap. 1-14]

After the death of Moses, God said to Joshua, "Be strong and of good courage! As I was with Moses, so I will be with you. Arise, go over this Jordan River, you and all your people, into the land that I am giving you. Do as I command and you will prosper."

So Joshua called the people from their tents. Twelve priests, carrying the Holy Ark on their shoulders, led the way down to the river's banks. As soon as the soles of their feet touched the water, the flow of the river stopped. The waters coming down from the north stood up in a heap, and the priests and all the people with them walked across on dry ground.

When the kings of the Canaanite cities of the neighborhood heard that God had done this great wonder for the people of Israel, all their courage melted away.

The armies of Israel felt themselves strong and ready for the stiffest of battles. Had not God at last removed the disgrace of their long slavery in Egypt? Had he not dried up the waters of the Jordan for Joshua, their new leader, just as years before he had dried up the Red Sea for Moses?

The excited Israelites made camp east of the walled city of Jericho and waited for God's directions. The message came to Joshua: "I am giving you this great city, its king and all its mighty men. Follow my directions faithfully and you will be rewarded. Do not try to scale the walls, or look for a weak spot or search for

57

some secret passageway. Instead simply lead your soldiers in a procession in broad daylight around the walls. Let the holy ark be carried at the head of the procession, with seven priests following in single file, each carrying a silver trumpet. Then let all the hosts of Israel march behind. Let no sound be made, no song be sung, and let no trumpet be blown until I command it."

Joshua did as God directed. At dawn the next morning this quiet procession marched around the city walls seven times. Each morning for five more days the same quiet procession was repeated. On the seventh morning, as they started on their seventh round, the signal came. The priests blew their silver trumpets and all the people shouted.

And, lo, the walls of the city of Jericho came tumbling down before their eyes! Immediately the Hebrew soldiers rushed over the fallen stones and into the city, killing as they went. Only one woman and her family were spared, because she had hidden Hebrew spies in her house at the risk of her own safety, and had thus saved them from capture. To complete the destruction, the soldiers set fire to the city, turning it into a heap of rubble and ashes.

Because of this, fear of Joshua's army spread far and wide over the land of Canaan. As they marched on farther into the country, city after city surrendered to them. Here and there they were defeated, but these failures were always because one or more persons among them had disobeyed God's clear commands. Perhaps some greedy captain hid valuable loot to use for his own benefit. Not until he had been punished would God help his people in battle again. Only when they obeyed God's commands were the armies of Israel victorious.

Two Centuries of Fighting for Canaan
[Judges chap. 1-16]

It took many years of fighting and hardship for the invading Israelites to conquer the land of Canaan. Indeed, in many towns they made friends with the Canaanites, contrary to God's instructions, and they settled down alongside them and began copying their manners and habits. These shepherds from the desert had many practical things to learn from the Canaanites. They did not know how to plow or plant barley and wheat, or how to care for vineyards and olive groves. They began to enjoy living in houses instead of tents. They liked the excitement of the village markets and the gaiety of the festival dances. They became curious about the gods the Canaanites worshiped and the shrines they had built on the tops of wooded hills where they saw the Canaanites bring their offerings and make their prayers. They were awed by the temples in the larger towns and by the ceremonies the priests performed before their idols. Soon the people of Israel were bringing their gifts to these gods of the Canaanites.

God had warned his people against these temptations, and he punished them from time to time for their disobedience. Sometimes he allowed them to be defeated in battle; sometimes he withheld the rains that made the crops grow, and sometimes he sent contagious diseases which spread among them and caused many to die. Yet always whenever their condition became desperate, God would have pity on them and inspire some brave chieftain to lead them into battle, and he would give these men more than human power over their enemies.

There was Gideon, for example, who, with one hundred men, armed merely with torches and trumpets, surprised a large camp of Midianites in the middle of the night and put them to flight.

And there was the giant Samson who, without a weapon of any kind, tore a young lion asunder; who took revenge on the

Philistines by slaying a thousand of their men with the jaw-bone of an ass; and who later, although himself a prisoner and blind, pulled down the main pillars of a Philistine temple, and thus in the hour of his own death destroyed three thousand of his enemies.

The People Crown Their First King

[I Samuel chap. 8-10]

As the years passed and the people of Israel increased in numbers and in strength, they grew eager to have a king as the nations around them had, so that all their different tribes—now twelve in number—might be joined together in one strong nation. They asked Samuel, their wise old priest, who for years had been leading their ceremonies of worship in the shrine at Shiloh, to choose a king for them.

But Samuel did not think the plan was a good one, since he felt that God should be their only king. When the people pleaded with him again and again, Samuel went to the shrine and asked God what to do, and the answer came: "Listen to the people and choose a king for them, but warn them that if they have a king they will have to do as he commands and it may not be as pleasant as they think." God even showed Samuel the person to choose. He was Saul, a popular young man and a daring soldier.

When crowned king, Saul gathered an army such as the people of Israel had never had before. Time and again he led them successfully into battle against their neighbors. He fortified the town of Hebron and made it the capital of the nation by building a royal palace there for himself and his family.

But Canaanite enemies were still living to the north and the south, the east and the west, who would have liked to drive the whole nation of Israel out of the land. The strongest among these enemies were the Philistines, who lived to the west along the fertile plain beside the Mediterranean Sea.

David shouted: "I come to you in the name of the God of the armies of Israel."

The Philistine Giant Goliath Challenges the Armies of Israel

[I Samuel 17:1-58]

A Philistine army and an Israelite army were camped on opposite hillsides with a wide valley between them—each waiting for the other to make an attack. The terrible day of battle came when one morning the Israelites saw a Philistine giant walk down the mountain and across the valley toward their camp. He was protected by a heavy coat of iron. A metal helmet covered his head. In his hand he carried a spear that looked as heavy and long as a weaver's beam, and a slave ran ahead carrying a huge shield.

When within hearing distance of the Israelites, the giant stopped and shouted with a thundering voice, "Choose a man for yourselves and let him come down to me. If he is able to kill me, we shall become your slaves. If I kill him, you shall be our slaves."

The soldiers of Israel were terrified—even King Saul himself. None had the courage to face the giant until, to everyone's surprise, a young shepherd named David went to King Saul and offered to fight the giant. King Saul hesitated to let the young man take the risk, but no one else would offer. King Saul tried to persuade David to wear his own coat of armor and carry his shield, but David refused. He was not used to such things. He insisted on going forth in his ordinary shepherd's clothes, taking nothing but his sling and a bag of stones.

When the giant, Goliath, saw this unprotected, slight young fellow coming forth to fight, he felt insulted. "Am I a dog," he shouted, "that you come to me with sticks?"

"I come to you in the name of the God of the armies of Israel whom you have challenged," shouted David. "This day he will deliver you into my hands."

David then ran hurriedly toward the giant, took a stone out

of the bag at his side, and slung it with such precise aim that it struck the giant on his forehead and he fell on his face to the ground.

When the Philistines saw that their champion was dead, they ran away in a panic. The army of Israel raised a great shout and chased after them. Thousands of the Philistines were killed.

Such an amazing victory so impressed the Israelites that as they were returning home to King Saul's capital city, the women ran out into the streets to meet them, playing on tambourines and cymbals and dancing and singing:

> Saul has slain his thousands
> But David his ten thousands.

That day David became the most popular hero of his people.

The Beginning of a Great Friendship

[I Samuel chap. 18-31; II Samuel chap. 1]

That day was also the beginning of a great friendship between David and King Saul's oldest son, Jonathan. He was so impressed with David's bravery and skill before the giant that he asked for the privilege of bringing David home to the palace. Soon the young hero was being treated as if he were one of the royal family, and everyone was pleased. Being skilled as a harpist, David led the entire household in many a pleasant evening of singing and dancing.

For a while all was well. King Saul treated the young giant-killer with respect and kindness. But slowly there grew in Saul's heart feelings of jealousy and fear lest David might become so popular that some day he would be powerful enough to try to usurp the throne.

As the months passed this jealousy grew. King Saul began being unpleasant to David at the table. He would fly into a rage without any real provocation. At such times the family said, "An evil spirit from God has entered into King Saul." These mad tantrums would frighten the entire household. Once King Saul even threw a spear across the room at David. Strange to say, David was the only one who could quiet the king at times like these; he did it by playing the old melodies he used to play as he watched his sheep on the hillside above Bethlehem.

Months and years passed. King Saul's jealousy grew into hate. He tried to find a way to have David killed without offending the people with whom he was so popular. He even commanded his son Jonathan to plot David's death in battle. But Jonathan remained loyal to his friend even at the risk of his own life; however, David had to stay in hiding for many months.

Finally God would no longer help the angry and frightened king. Saul was no longer able, therefore, to be a successful military leader. His armies met defeats rather than victories. In the end both King Saul and his son Jonathan were slain on the same day and in the same battle.

When David was told the news of their death, he wept bitterly and long. "The glory of Israel has departed!" he cried. In the loss of his faithful friend Jonathan, David felt even more bereaved than if he had lost a lover and wife.

The Glory of David's Kingdom

[II Samuel chap. 5-24]

Upon Saul's death, David became king of Israel. Of all the rulers that that nation ever had, none has been so honored as King David. His long reign of forty years marks the period of Israel's most renowned greatness. He enlarged the boundaries of his country by subduing cities up to then unconquered. The most important among these was the fortress city of Jerusalem, which he later made his capital. Even to this day, Jerusalem is called the City of David.

There he built a palace larger and more elaborate than King

Saul had had in Hebron. David would also have liked to build a great temple to God, but he was kept too busy fighting battles to build a temple. He did, however, set up a large tent on a hilltop in the center of Jerusalem where the ark could be kept and where God was worshiped. In this way Jerusalem became not only the capital city where King David and his royal family lived, but also the center of holy worship for all the people.

King Solomon's Glory and Tragedy
[I Kings chap. 2-10; 11:1-43]

When King David was old and about to die, he called his chosen son, Solomon, to him and charged him, saying, "Solomon, my son, be strong, and show yourself a man. Serve the Lord with all your heart. Happy as I have been to have the ark here in Jerusalem, I have not felt right about living in a fine palace myself and having the holy ark still sitting in a tent. When you become king in my place, build a great and glorious temple to God so that his name may be honored over all the earth."

King David gave Solomon a model of the kind of temple he had dreamed of. He charted its size and the shape of its different rooms and courts. He described all the golden bowls, lamps, curtains, candlesticks, and altars that should be in it. "Do not be discouraged, Solomon," he said, "by the great labor. Seek the help of my good friend, King Hiram of Tyre, and ask him to send you his skilled workers. Know that God will not fail you until all the work has been completed."

On King David's death, Solomon had to fight his brothers for the throne, but he finally won the crown. During his long reign he enlarged the kingdom till it reached from the far north to the far south near the boundaries of Egypt, and from the Euphrates River on the east to the land of the Philistines on the west. After these victories the people had peace "on all sides round about."

King Solomon became famous as the wisest man in all the world. He composed three thousand proverbs and wrote over a thousand songs. Men traveled from many lands to listen to his wisdom.

He became very rich, too. He owned forty thousand stalls of horses and thousands of chariots. He employed thousands of lumbermen and miners and stonecutters. He also hired many craftsmen, skilled in working with bronze and silver and gold, to make pillars and basins, bowls and lamp sticks. He built a fleet of ships on the shores of the Red Sea and manned them with merchants and sailors who sailed to the Far East and brought back treasures of silver, gold, and ivory, and monkeys and peacocks.

King Solomon also built a new palace for himself, his family and servants, and filled it with the finest of furniture. Even all his plates and drinking vessels were of gold. He built a grand throne in the large hall of judgment. Six steps led up to the throne. On either side of each step was the statue of a lion. And the whole throne and all the lions were overlaid with gold.

As his father, David, had directed, King Solomon also built a large and wonderful temple to God, with walls and floors overlaid with gold. The small inner chamber—the holy of holies, where the ark was placed—was entirely covered with gold. It took twenty years of labor to complete both the palace and the temple. When the temple was completed, thousands of people came up to Jerusalem to celebrate the event, and thousands of oxen and sheep were slain on the altar and the people feasted in the large open court.

After this great festival, God appeared to Solomon in a dream and said, "If now you will live day by day with a true and good heart and if you will do all that I command you to do, I will bless you and your people. And if your children after you will also obey my word, then I will make your kingdom everlasting. No one shall be able to destroy you. But if you go and serve other gods and worship them, then I will cut you and your people off from this land, and this temple shall become a heap of ruins. Everyone passing by will be astonished and remember your people with scorn."

But as King Solomon grew in wealth and power, he began to lose his desire to walk humbly with God. Instead he became absorbed in his own personal pleasure. He married one beautiful princess and chieftain's daughter after another until he had seven hundred wives, some of them foreigners who worshiped other gods. King Solomon even built shrines for their gods and went with his wives to worship. So his heart was turned away from the God who had brought his people out of the land of Egypt. Twice God warned King Solomon: "Since you have not kept your promise to me, I will tear the kingdom away from your son when he comes to the throne. For the sake of David, your good father, and for the sake of Jerusalem and the temple, I will allow your descendants to have just this small southern part. Ten out of your twelve tribes will rebel and set up another kingdom."

The Kingdom is Divided
[I Kings 12:1-24]

Immediately after King Solomon's death, Jeroboam, one of the captains of his laboring squads, started a rebellion. Ten out of the twelve tribes that made up the nation followed Jeroboam. He set up a new kingdom in the north, with Samaria as the capital city; Solomon's son, Rehoboam, was left with only two small tribes in the south and the city of Jerusalem for his capital. Thus the Hebrew nation was divided into two kingdoms, the northern one being called Israel and the southern one Judah, and there was war between the two kings, Jeroboam and Rehoboam, continually, as long as they lived.

Many Kings Make Israel Sinful
[I Kings 12:25-33; chap. 13; 16:1-29]

The history of the following three hundred and fifty years is a story full of much wrong-doing, tragedy, and war. Not a single one of the kings who ruled in the northern kingdom and only a few of those in the south did what was right in the sight of God.

Jeroboam, the first king in the north, knew that it would be unwise to let his people go down to Jerusalem in the southern kingdom in order to worship in the great temple there. So he built two smaller temples in his own kingdom, one in Dan in the northern part, and one in Bethel in the south. In each of these temples, King Jeroboam placed a golden idol of a bull and said to the people, "Behold your God which brought you out of the land of Egypt!" King Jeroboam made other shrines, also, on the tops of many hills, in which he placed other images of God. He put priests in charge of these different shrines to receive the people's sacrifices and to lead them in their prayers.

So King Jeroboam required his people to disobey the commandment of God against idols. For twenty-two years he reigned, and all the while he led his people in wrong-doing. After Jeroboam's death, his son Nadab ruled, but in two years' time he and all his brothers were murdered, and the murderer seized the throne. During the next half century, one insurrection followed another. Each new king instructed his people to worship the idols set up in the shrines, just as King Jeroboam had done. So God's anger was kindled like a burning flame against his people.

Of all the kings that ruled in Samaria after King Jeroboam, the worst was Ahab; and it was Ahab's Canaanite queen, Jezebel, who led him into his great sinning. For her sake King Ahab built a new temple in Samaria, not to the glory of the God of Israel, but for the worship of Baal, the great god of the Canaanites. Ahab even hired hundreds of priests to help the people in their worship of the god Baal.

Elijah — The Great Man of God

[I Kings 17:1-24]

But there were in Israel a few men who remained loyal to God and his commands. The greatest of these was Elijah, a bold preacher from the country on the other side of the Jordan River. He warned King Ahab, saying, "There shall be neither dew nor rain in all your land for three years—or until God himself gives the word—or until you and the people repent and are ready to turn from your evil ways."

King Ahab hated Elijah for saying this, and tried to lay hold of him to kill him; but God hid Elijah in the wild country beyond the river and told the ravens to feed him. So the ravens brought wild berries and fruits to Elijah in their bills and laid them at his feet. These were his bread and meat morning and evening, and the little brook in the canyon gave him fresh water to drink.

Sometimes Elijah begged food from the people of the nearby town. Once he asked a widow for a piece of bread and a drink of water.

"As truly as God lives," she said, "I have nothing in my house, except a small handful of meal in a jar and a small bottle of oil. I am just now going out to gather some sticks to make a fire so that I can bake a few cakes for me and my son to eat. When these are gone we will have to starve."

To her surprise, Elijah said, "Don't be afraid. Go and do as I say. For I hear God saying to me, 'That jar of meal shall not be used up and that bottle of oil shall last until the day I send rain again on the land.' "

The woman did as Elijah said, and she and her son and Elijah all ate for many days. No matter how often she took meal from the jar, the meal was never spent and the supply of oil never failed.

Again there was a time when the widow's son became very sick, and before long there was no breath left in him at all. He was dead. The widow blamed Elijah. "What have you against me, O man of God, that you have brought this punishment on me?"

"Give me your boy," said Elijah. And he carried him to his own room upstairs and laid him down on the bed.

Then Elijah cried out to God in prayer. "O Lord my God, have you brought this calamity on the widow who has been so kind to me? It cannot be."

Elijah then lay down on the bed with the boy and placed his mouth upon the boy's mouth and breathed into his nostrils his own living breath. As he did so, Elijah prayed that the soul of the boy might come back into his body.

Presently the boy began breathing again, and Elijah picked him up and carried him downstairs alive, to his mother's great joy. "Now I know," said the mother, "that you are a man of God and that what you speak is the truth."

King Ahab Pouts and Jezebel Plots

[I Kings 21:1-29]

King Ahab in his elaborate palace knew nothing of what Elijah was doing or where he was. He was glad to forget him for a while.

Now there was a farmer, named Naboth, who owned a vineyard not far from Ahab's palace in Samaria. As Ahab began planning how to enlarge his palace ground, he decided he would like to have a vegetable garden just where Naboth had his vineyard.

So the king sent word to Naboth to ask him to sell his vineyard, or, if he preferred, to accept a better vineyard somewhere else in exchange for it. But Naboth did not want to sell his vineyard, even to a king. It had belonged to his father and his grandfather and even before that it had belonged in the family.

Ahab was angered when he received Naboth's proud answer. Like a spoiled child he went off to his bedroom and lay down on his bed and turned away his face, and would eat no food.

Queen Jezebel was amazed to see her husband pouting about something he wanted and thought he could not have. When she heard what the trouble was, she said, "Aren't you the King of Israel? Get up and be cheerful. I will get the vineyard for you."

So the wicked queen began to plot how Naboth might be gotten rid of. She wrote letters to a number of the chief men of Naboth's town, and signed the letters with the king's name. She accused Naboth of having cursed God and the king, and wrote ordering them to put him on trial. The result of her plot was that these men took Naboth outside the city and stoned him to death. As soon as King Ahab heard that Naboth was dead he went down to the vineyard and claimed it as his.

Then God appeared to the prophet Elijah and said, "Go down to meet King Ahab. He is in Naboth's vineyard. He has killed the owner in order to get the vineyard."

When King Ahab saw Elijah, he said, "Have you found me, O my enemy?" "I have found you," said Elijah, "because you have sold yourself to do what is evil. God will bring evil upon you; he will utterly sweep you away. None of your sons will ever be king; as the dogs licked up the blood of Naboth, so they will lick up your blood—and Jezebel's, too." But King Ahab did not listen, nor did he change his plans.

Three Years' Famine and the Contest on Mount Carmel
[I Kings 18:1-46; II Kings 2:1-12]

As a punishment God continued to keep the rains from falling over the land of Israel. The brooks dried up, rivers became little streams, crops would not grow, fruit did not ripen on the trees; men were dying of hunger. King Ahab was worried.

One day he and Elijah met by the roadside. Elijah was ready. God had told him just what to do. So Elijah said to the King, "Send and gather a large assembly of people on Mount Carmel. Bring also all the four hundred and fifty priests of the god Baal who are serving you. Let us make a test and see who is really God."

So King Ahab gathered the people and the priests of Baal on Mount Carmel. Elijah with his small company of followers also came. When all was ready, Elijah spoke to the great assembly. "How long will you go limping between two beliefs? If the Lord is God, follow him, but if Baal is God, follow *him*."

"These are good words," said the people one to another.

So the priests of Baal chose a bullock, killed and prepared it as an offering and laid it on their altar, but they put no fire under it. "Baal will send the fire," they said.

From early morning until noon, the priests danced and called to Baal. "O Baal, hear us!" they cried over and over. "Accept our offering. Send us a sign. Send down fire from the sky." But no voice was heard in answer.

Noon came and Elijah began mocking them, "Cry louder! Perhaps Baal is off on a journey or he may be asleep and must be awakened." The priests cried louder. They danced more violently. They even cut themselves with swords till blood ran down their bodies. Late afternoon came, and still no answer.

Elijah then said it was his turn. He built another altar. He made a trench around it, and placed wood and a slain bullock on the altar. Then he took four jars of water and poured them over the sacrifice. He did this a second and even a third time until the sacrifice was drenched and water filled the trench.

Elijah then stood beside the altar and prayed, "O God of Abraham, Isaac, and Jacob, let it be known this day that I am your servant and that you are God."

Presently fire from the Lord fell down from the sky. It licked up the water in the trench and burned the wood and the sacrifice.

When the people standing by saw this happen, they fell to the ground on their faces and cried, "The Lord he is God. The Lord he is God."

Presently a second sign was given. First a small cloud the size of a man's hand was seen in the sky. Soon the wind began to blow and in a little while the whole sky became black with clouds. A heavy rain poured down.

Both terrified and happy, the people rushed down the mountain toward their homes. King Ahab found his chariot and drove furiously back to his palace, while Elijah wound his robes about his waist and ran through the rain back into hiding.

In spite of these and other great signs from God, King Ahab and his queen did not change their way of life. Finally the threat which Elijah had made years before came true. King Ahab was killed in battle, and Queen Jezebel was thrown from a window and her corpse left unburied to be eaten by dogs.

Elijah, the daring prophet, pleased God so greatly that God did not let him die as other men die. Instead, when Elijah was old and ready to die God sent down from the sky a chariot of fire driven by horses of fire, and Elijah was carried in this chariot by a whirlwind up into heaven, and was seen no more.

Israel's Tragic End

[II Kings 17:1-41; Amos; Hosea]

God sent other prophets to the kings of Israel to warn them, saying, "Turn from your evil ways and keep the commandments I have given you." But the people were stubborn and would not listen. They made images of wood and metal, and worshiped the Canaanite Baal. The rich dealt cruelly with the poor. Judges were not just and fair in their decisions. Too many people cared more for the show of rich living and the pomp of the festivals than they did for coming before God with clean and honest hearts. The prophet Amos came from his sheep herding and warned them of God's anger. The prophet Hosea pleaded with his people to be true to God as a woman is true to her husband. "He desires goodness from you more than sacrifices," Hosea declared.

But the kings of Israel and their people abused or killed their prophets and refused to change their ways. Finally God determined to put an end to the kingdom of Israel.

Now to the southeast of Israel was a strong nation called Assyria. God allowed its king to send a great army against the city of Samaria. It camped in a circle around the walls of the city for three long years. No one could go into the city to sell food, and none could go out to gather the fruits of their farms. The people within the walls were slowly starving to death. At last, realizing they had to give up or all die of starvation, they hoisted the flag of surrender and the gates were opened to the enemy. With great cruelty the Assyrian army killed many of the people and plundered the palaces and temples; they took captive men, women and children by the thousands, compelling them to leave their homes and go to serve as slaves in foreign lands. So ten of the twelve tribes of Israel were scattered abroad and were never able to establish a kingdom again.

King David's City Too Becomes a Heap of Ruins

[II Kings chap. 18-24; 25:1-30; II Chronicles 36:1-21; Isaiah; Jeremiah]

In the Kingdom of Judah to the south during these two hundred and more years, there were a few kings who did right in the sight of God and who worshiped him alone, but there were many more kings who followed after the gods of the Canaanites and who worshiped idols of wood and stone.

The news of the destruction of Samaria was a shock to the people of Jerusalem, for they feared that the king of Assyria might march against them next. In fact it was but ten years later that another king of Assyria did besiege the city of Jerusalem with thousands of fighting men. But the good King Hezekiah was on the throne at that time, and God would not allow the Assyrians to conquer. So at a time when the Assyrian army was confident of a quick victory, God sent an angel down from heaven in the middle of the night. The angel slew a hundred and eighty-five thousand of the Assyrian soldiers camping outside the walls of Jerusalem. In the morning, when the few who were left alive rose and found dead bodies all around them, they pulled up their tents in fright and hurried back home. So Jerusalem was saved.

But King Hezekiah was followed on the throne by sons and grandsons who did evil in the sight of the Lord and who made the people of Judah sin. So God decided he would no longer protect Judah from its enemies.

In the meantime Assyria itself had been conquered by King Nebuchadnezzar of Babylon. As soon as he had made himself strong in this former country of the Assyrians, King Nebuchadnezzar sent his armies against Jerusalem. The first time they besieged the city, the king in Jerusalem made peace with him by consenting to pay tribute to Babylon. But when this king in

Jerusalem died, his son decided to rebel and to fight the Babylonians.

The Babylonian army returned to Jerusalem, made an opening in the city walls, and took the city. They slew thousands of the people and led tens of thousands of others away as captives to the land of Babylon, where they were forced to do hard labor. The Babylonian armies plundered the temple and the king's palace, carrying off everything made of silver or gold or bronze. They even scraped the gold covering off the walls and floors and holy altars and tables. They killed all the king's sons while they forced the king to watch. Then they put out the king's eyes, bound him, and led him off to a Babylonian prison. The Babylonian soldiers also set fire to the temple and the palace, and hundreds of the best houses of the city went up in flames. They even knocked down the city walls. Thus the proud city of David became a pile of rubbish where jackals prowled; only a few of the poorest peasants were left to wander hungrily through the ruins, gathering food from deserted gardens and vineyards.

But the Hope of Greatness Survived

[Ezra; Nehemiah; Isaiah (especially 11:6-9); Ezekiel; Psalm 137]

The Hebrew captives in the mighty city of Babylon felt lonely, discouraged, and disgraced. As they labored, they often passed the palaces and temples of Babylon, but instead of being impressed when they looked up at the famous hanging gardens and pyramid-like temples, their hearts were filled with sorrow. In the evening after work they would sit on the banks of the Euphrates or beside one of the many canals that made the Euphrates plain a garden. They would bring their harps with them, expecting to sing the old songs they used to sing in Jerusalem, but instead they would hang their harps on the willow trees and sit down by the water and weep.

Seventy long years passed. A few courageous and hopeful ones among them talked of returning to Jerusalem. They appealed to King Cyrus to allow a few to go back. With Nehemiah as leader, some did return and begin to rebuild the walls of Jerusalem and to repair the temple. Small and plain though this rebuilt temple was, the people began to regain their courage. They truly tried to do what they thought was right in the sight of God.

A few great leaders among them became convinced that some day Jerusalem would be more glorious than it had ever been even in the days of King Solomon. They said the promise which God had given to Abraham, Isaac, and Jacob would some day come true. "God has been teaching us through our suffering," they said. "Now if only we will do justly and obey God and worship him, we shall again be his 'chosen people,' and through us God will bless all the nations on the earth."

These prophets said that Jerusalem would some day be the capital not merely of the nation of Israel, but the capital of the whole world. A king would sit on the throne in Jerusalem who would be greater than any king that had ever been. All the nations of the world would come and bow down before this king of all kings. And his kingdom would be everlasting. None could ever overthrow it, because the king in this kingdom would be one sent from heaven by God himself—an immortal, divine king, a messiah, who would rule forever.

So the people of Israel began to dream of a time when all wars would cease. Men would melt their swords and make them into plows and pruning hooks. When this dream of a world-wide and everlasting kingdom of goodness came true, even the animals would be friendly with each other. The wolf would lie down peacefully with the lamb, and the leopard with the kid; the calf and the young lion would be friends, and a little child would not be afraid to walk and talk with them. The cow and the bear would feed together, and the lion and the wolf would eat straw like the ox; nobody would hurt anybody, and the whole world would be filled with the knowledge of God as water fills the sea.

But years and centuries passed and there was no sign that this wonderful dream would come true. In fact, many of the descendants of the Hebrews who had been led away to Babylon as captives were still held in Babylon and forced to do hard labor for their masters.

Those who had returned to the land of their ancestors were few, and they were never able to make their nation strong. One after another, neighboring peoples sent armies into this little country and conquered it. After the Babylonians came the Persians; after the Persians came the Greeks; and after the Greeks came the mighty Romans. From time to time brave Hebrew warriors led their people into battle against their enemies; but their victories were small, and in the end they were always defeated. For nearly six hundred years, God's "chosen people" were ruled by foreign conquerors.

So the Fifth Great Age of Time ended in much sorrow; but a hope glowed through the sorrow, like a thin sunbeam shining through a crack into a dark room.

The Sixth Great Age of Time

God Decides on the Great Sacrifice

Over and over again God had tried to help his "chosen people," but they continued to be rebellious. They followed other gods and refused to deal justly with their neighbors.

A just and good God could not allow such wickedness to go unpunished, yet he so loved the world that he could not endure the thought that the people he had created would have to be destroyed. He longed to give back immortality to men. But first the people of the world must be shown the terrible nature of their sinning. Some very great sacrifice must be made. Even though thousands of animals might be sacrificed as burnt offerings, these would not be enough. Even though men, women, and children might be sacrificed, these would not be a sufficient ransom. Someone worth more than all the people of the whole world put together must become a substitute sacrifice. Who was there worthy of such a supreme mission? There was but one person. It must be God's only Son, who had been living at God's right hand in heaven from all eternity—even before the world was.

The Son of God Is Sent from Heaven

[Matthew 1:18-25; 2:1-12; Luke 1:26-38; Philippians 2:5-11]

So God sent his only Son down from heaven, that all men might live through him. But this Holy One did not come to earth in his Godlike form. Just as other babies grow in their mothers'

79

wombs before birth, so the Son of God grew in the womb of a woman of Israel, named Mary, whom God chose out of all the women of the world to be the mother of his Son. Now Mary was engaged to a man named Joseph, but they were not yet married when this divine child was born. Although Mary and Joseph were married later and had other children, Joseph was not the father of this first-born son. Jesus' father was God himself. Before his birth, Mary was told by an angel that her son was to be very great, the king of an everlasting kingdom. He was the Holy Son of God, the Messiah, the Savior of the world.

Since this babe was born in the same manner as other children, and since he was the child of an unknown peasant woman, it was important that God give signs to show others beside Mary that this new child was truly his only Son from heaven.

God therefore sent angels to tell of the birth of the Holy One. Shepherds keeping watch by night over their flocks saw an angel in the sky above them, and they were frightened. But the angel said, "Be not afraid; for I bring you good tidings of great joy which shall be for all people: for there is born this day in the city of David the longed-for Messiah—Christ the Lord. You will find him wrapped in swaddling clothes and lying in a manger."

Suddenly there was with the angel a host of angels, singing joyful praises.

> Glory to God in the highest,
> And on earth peace among men in whom he is
>   well pleased.

Then the angels disappeared and the light in the sky faded. The shepherds hastened to Bethlehem. They found the babe lying in a manger with his mother beside him, and they told Mary and Joseph all that had happened. Those who heard their story wondered greatly. Mary pondered their words quietly in her heart.

Another sign came when a new star shone in the sky with a special brightness. Wise men of the East, accustomed to studying the meanings of changes in the sky, observed the star and said, "It is a sign. The King of the Jews has been born."

Immediately, the three wise men set out for Bethlehem. And lo, the star they had seen went before them, leading the way until it stood over the place where the young child was.

When the wise men came into the house and saw the young child with his mother, they fell on their faces and worshiped him. Opening their treasure-chests, they offered him gifts—gold, frank-incense, and myrrh.

During all his childhood years, Jesus lived, unnoticed by the general public, in the simple home of Joseph, the carpenter of the village of Nazareth. Like the other children in the village, he was obedient to his parents. He grew in both size and strength, as well as in wisdom. He became a favorite with the neighbors, and the special favor of God was with him.

Jesus Learns He Is God's Son

[Matthew 3:1-17; Luke 3:1-22]

It was not until he was grown that Jesus came to realize that he was God's special divine Son sent from heaven to be the Savior of the world. This is how it was shown to him.

A preacher, whom the people called John the Baptist, was being talked about all over Palestine. He was a robust, out-of-door man who lived in the desert country near the Jordan River. He wore the skins of animals and ate such food as the desert afforded —for instance, locusts and wild honey.

But John the Baptist was more than a hermit. He was a preacher sent from God to announce the coming of the Son of God into the world, and to call people to repent and be ready. John's preaching was so startling and impressive that hundreds left their homes and walked long distances into the desert in order to listen to him.

John said, "Repent, every one of you. Give up your sins, whatever they are. Change your ways of life. If you have two coats, give one of them to a person who has none. If you have taken more interest on your money than you should have done, stop stealing from others. If you are a soldier, stop your violence, and do not demand anything from another wrongfully. The divine king, for whose coming our people have been longing these many years, is coming soon. Repent and be ready to have a part in his kingdom. God is like a woodsman ready with his axe. The trees that are not bringing forth good fruit he will cut down and burn. He will spare only the good trees. Be like good trees and bring forth the good fruit of good deeds."

When some were ready to promise to change their ways, John the Baptist led them down into the Jordan and baptized them. It was a sign that they had been washed clean of their sins.

One day Jesus was among John's listeners, and after the preaching he went up to John and said, "I want you to baptize me."

But John the Baptist tried to hinder him, for John knew that Jesus was the Holy One about whose coming he had been preaching. "I have need to be baptized by you," he said to Jesus. "Why do you come to me?"

But Jesus urged John until he consented.

As Jesus, after his baptism, was coming up out of the water, God's sign came. The sky opened and the Spirit of God descended in the form of a dove and rested above his head. And Jesus heard a voice coming out of heaven, saying, "You are my beloved Son. I am well pleased with you."

At that great moment Jesus knew that he was not a man like other men, but that he was God's only Son, who once had lived in heaven with God. It was an awesome experience. What could it really mean? He must be alone to think it through. So he hurried away from the crowds and off into the desert. He could not help it. He felt driven by the spirit of God in him.

The Devil Tempts the Son of God

[Matthew 4:1-11; Mark 1:12-13; Luke 4:1-13]

For six weeks — forty days — Jesus stayed in the desert alone, fasting all the while.

In the meantime, the devil was waiting, for he knew that this Jesus was the Son of God, sent down from heaven to save mankind. He followed Jesus into the desert, and one day showed himself to Jesus.

"If you are really the Son of God," said the devil, "why do you go hungry? Command these stones to turn into bread."

Jesus looked at the devil and said firmly, "Man shall not live by bread alone."

The devil then led Jesus up to the top of the highest pinnacle of the temple. "If you are the Son of God," said the devil, "you should be able to throw yourself down from here and not be hurt. You surely remember the words in the scriptures promising that angels will hold you up and keep you from being dashed to pieces."

Jesus again answered the devil firmly. "The scriptures say also that one must not tempt God."

The devil tried a third time. He led Jesus up to the top of a very high mountain where he could look about and see all the kingdoms of the world. "All these kingdoms I will give you," said the devil, "if you will kneel down and worship me."

"Get behind me, Satan!" cried Jesus. "In the scriptures it is written: 'You shall worship the Lord your God and him only you shall serve.' "

The devil then left Jesus, and angels came and cared for him.

Jesus Becomes a Traveling Preacher
[Mark 1:14-45; 6:1-6; Luke 4:14-44; 5:1-15]

After these rigorous weeks in the wilderness, Jesus returned to his home town of Nazareth. He tried to tell his neighbors about his experiences. Sometimes he spoke in the village synagogue. He told his friends that he believed he had been sent by God to preach good news to those who were in trouble, and to tell them that the kingdom of God was near at hand.

But his neighbors took offense at what Jesus said. Scornfully they asked, "Isn't this the son of the carpenter? Where does he get the authority to say these things?"

So Jesus left his home town and spent the next three years traveling from one town to another throughout Palestine, preaching his good news to those who would listen. Sometimes they would gather by the shore of the Sea of Galilee. Sometimes they sat in the courtyard of a friend's house, sometimes in the market place, or in the synagogue, or out in the country on a hillside. Wherever Jesus was and people wanted to hear him, he would speak.

Before long a small group of disciples followed him around wherever he went. Sometimes the listening crowds reached into the thousands. The fame of his preaching grew until the whole countryside was talking about the man from Nazareth. And they were asking, "Who is he? What is this he is saying? He speaks with authority."

What Was Jesus Saying?
[Matthew 5:1-16; 18:1-6; Mark 1:14, 15; John 4:24; 12:46]

Like John the Baptist, Jesus called people to repent of their evil ways. "The longed-for kingdom of God is near at hand. Believe me and repent," he said. "But God's kingdom is not the kind most of you are thinking of. The kingdom of God is a kingdom without a throne or a palace. The king who rules this kingdom is in heaven. He is God himself, and he rules in the hearts of men. God is a spirit, and they that worship him must worship in spirit and truth. Only those who love God and love their neighbors too can belong in this kingdom. Those who do what God commands, not those who *say* they are going to obey God, can belong in this kingdom. God does not call the proud or those who think themselves more righteous than others. Only those who are humble as little children can enter God's kingdom.

"God's kingdom is not for Jews only. The gates to the kingdom are open to all—the wise and the foolish, the rich and the poor, Jews and Gentiles.

"I have been sent by God to proclaim this good news," said Jesus. "I am like a light sent from God to show men how to live. Anyone who will believe in me and who will follow me, shall live forever. Even though he die, yet he shall live again in heaven with God and the holy angels.

"Blessed are the poor in spirit; for theirs is the kingdom of heaven.

"Blessed are the merciful for they shall obtain mercy.

"Blessed are the peacemakers; for they shall be called sons of God."

The common people heard Jesus gladly and wondered at the gracious words that he spoke.

Jesus Performs Miraculous Wonders
[Mark 6:30-56; John 6:1-40]

Five thousand people had been hanging on Jesus' words all day long. They had followed him across the Lake of Galilee and were far from their homes. They had eaten nothing since early morning, and they were tired and hungry.

"How much food have we among us?" asked Jesus. Going through the crowd, the disciples could find but one person with food, and he was a lad with only five loaves and two small fishes.

"Everybody sit down," said Jesus. He then took the five loaves in his hand, and prayed over them. He broke them in pieces and gave them to his twelve disciples to distribute among the crowd.

He held up the two fishes also, prayed over them, and gave them to his disciples to distribute. As the food was passed and pieces were taken one by one, new pieces miraculously appeared in their places in the basket, so that every one had all he wanted to eat. When gathering up what was left over, the twelve disciples found that each one of them still had a basketful of bread.

When the people had seen this great wonder happen before their eyes, they wanted at once to crown Jesus King of the Jews. But Jesus, realizing that such a thing would be unwise, withdrew quietly into the woods and up the mountainside, where he stayed hidden and alone until after it was dark.

The amazed and puzzled crowd finally scattered to their homes. The twelve disciples went down to the lake shore and got into their boat and started across the lake; suddenly a strong wind began to blow and the lake became very rough.

They had rowed three or four miles from shore when they saw some one coming toward them through the darkness. To their great surprise, they soon discovered it was Jesus walking over the top of the water as if it were dry land. They were frightened.

"Don't be afraid," called Jesus. "It is I." The disciples recognized his voice, and when he was beside their boat they took him into it. Immediately they were on the other side of the lake.

In the morning a number of people sought Jesus out and began asking him to explain what had happened the day before. Jesus answered, "It means this. I am the bread of life; he who believes in me shall never hunger or thirst. I have come down from heaven, not to do my own will, but the will of him that sent me. And this is the will of my Father, that every one who sees the Son and believes in him shall have eternal life, and I will raise him up at the last day."

Jesus Made Enemies As Well As Followers

[Mark 2:23-28; 3:1-6]

Some took offense at the things Jesus said and did. There were several reasons for this. For example, the kind of goodness that Jesus said belongs in the kingdom of God is a goodness of the feelings as well as a goodness of good deeds done. Jesus, therefore, sometimes set aside some of the strict rules that the teachers of his time thought most important because he felt there were other more important matters. For instance, Jesus refused to be bound by the Jewish laws regarding the things that must not be done on the Sabbath day. When he and his disciples were hungry, they picked wheat from the standing stalks in the field even though it was the Sabbath. Jesus even did some of his miracle healings in the synagogues on the Sabbath. He stopped his sermon one Sabbath morning and healed a man whose arm had been withered and paralyzed for years. At this the leaders of the synagogue became "filled with madness."

On another Sabbath day Jesus made a man well who had been bedridden for thirty-eight years. Again and again friends had carried him down to a certain pool in Jerusalem in the hope of his being cured, if only he could get into the pool first after the spring began to bubble. But some one else always got in first and was the only one healed. Jesus had pity on the helpless man, and spoke to him kindly. He said to him simply, "Take up your bed and walk." Immediately the man realized he was well. He arose, picked up his bed, and walked home praising God.

But the Jewish law was against carrying any kind of burden on the Sabbath day. Why couldn't Jesus heal people on some other day than the Sabbath? Because of these and other such healings, some of the leading men of the synagogues began to plot how they might kill Jesus without bringing down on their heads the anger of the multitudes that hailed him as one sent from God.

Jesus Foreknew His Death and Resurrection
[Mark 10:32-34; Luke 18:31-34]

From the time when God first revealed to Jesus at his baptism that he was his only Son, sent to be the Savior of the world, Jesus knew that he would be hated and killed. He knew he would have to give his life as a ransom for the world's many sinners. Jesus knew also that death would not be the end. He knew that God would raise him from the dead and carry him back to heaven where he would sit at God's right hand through all eternity. All this Jesus told his disciples privately.

"The time will come," he said to them, "when the leaders of the people will turn me over to the Roman rulers, and they will condemn me to death. They will spit on me, and mock me, and whip me, and then they will crucify me on a cross. But do not be sad, for I came from heaven for this purpose—to give my life as a ransom for all who will believe in me and repent of their sins. This is God's will for me. I have come into the world not to do my own will, but to do the will of my Father who is in heaven.

"To prove to you that I am truly the Son of God, sent from heaven, God will show you a great wonder. After I have been in my grave for three days, I shall come forth out of the grave alive."

But his disciples were not able to believe him.

The Crowds Parade in Jesus' Honor
[Matthew 21:1-11; Mark 11:1-11; Luke 19:29-44]

It was springtime, just before the great Passover festival in Jerusalem. Jesus and his disciples were among the crowds coming from all over Palestine on their way to the city of David to join in the celebration. As the long line of pilgrims neared the city, the news was spread among them that their favorite teacher was with them. Quickly someone put Jesus on an ass, and made him ride at their head toward the city. As they entered the great gate, they shouted and sang and strewed the roadways with leafy branches and even with their own garments. This was their song:

Blessed is he that comes in the name of the Lord!
Blessed is the kingdom of our father David!
Blessed is the king that comes in the name of the Lord!
Praise God for all his mighty works—for the sick who
    have been healed;
For the lame who walk, for the blind who see, and for
    the dead who are alive again.
Peace in heaven and glory in the highest.

The whole city was stirred by the singing and the shouting. "Who is this?" the people asked, and the crowds answered, "This is the prophet Jesus, from Nazareth of Galilee."

The Riot in the Temple Court
[Matthew 21:12-17; Mark 11:15-19; John 2:13-22]

Jesus realized that such a demonstration of his popularity was dangerous. He knew the tragic fate in store for the people of Jerusalem. He could see the city being besieged by its enemies, its temple in ruins and its people slain. And he wept for his people. Alas, they did not know that the peace of the kingdom they were hoping for would not result from their setting him up as King.

As Jesus was entering Jerusalem, he realized too that the time of his own death was near. But he had committed himself to God's will and he would not turn back.

He went along with the other worshiping pilgrims into the large open court of the temple, where the Passover lambs and doves were to be purchased and turned over to the priests for sacrifice, and where every man was to pay the required temple tax of a Jewish shekel. Quickly the happy crowd turned to dickering and tongue-lashing. The merchants at their stalls were asking exorbitant prices for their lambs and doves. And the Jews from foreign lands, who had only foreign coins, had to pay twice what they should have in order to put the Jewish shekel in the offering boxes.

Jesus' anger was stirred. These temple officers were not interested in helping people to worship God. They were interested only in making money. This time Jesus was determined to protest, regardless of the danger. He made a whip of cords, and walked over to the men in their stalls. "Take these things away!" he cried. "My Father's house shall be called a house of prayer. You have made it a den of robbers." When they refused, Jesus turned over the tables of the money-changers.

When the chief priests in the temple and the principal men of the city heard of this riot in the temple court, they got together secretly to plot how they might get rid of this Jesus of Nazareth, for they were frightened when they saw how the crowds hung around him, listening with astonishment and awe to every word he spoke.

The Last Supper With His Disciples

[Matthew 26:17-29; Mark 14:12-29; Luke 22:7-38; John 13:1-38; I Corinthians 11:23-25]

When evening came, Jesus and his twelve disciples were eating the Passover supper together in an upstairs room in a Jerusalem home. The mood of the group was serious. They sensed danger, but hesitated to talk about it. Jesus alone understood fully what was about to happen. He opened the conversation at the table.

"One of you sitting here at the table with me is going to betray me," he said. The disciples were shocked. They could not believe him. "The time has come," Jesus continued. "This is the last supper I shall eat with you until we eat together in the kingdom of heaven."

Jesus then took a loaf of bread in his hand. After giving thanks, he broke it into pieces and as he passed them around, he said, "When you eat this bread, you are eating my body which I am about to give as a sacrifice for the sins of the world. Eat of it, all of you, that you may have a part in this sacrifice."

In the same way Jesus lifted a cup of wine and said, "This wine is my blood, shed for the sake of many. It is the new covenant I am making with God which I am sealing with my own blood in order that forgiveness may be granted to all who will believe.

"Whenever hereafter you gather together to break bread and to drink wine, do it in memory of me. In this way you will make known my death to all the world."

As soon as Judas had drunk his wine, the devil entered into him. Jesus, understanding what had happened, said quietly to him, "What you are going to do, do quickly." Immediately Judas left the table and went out into the night alone.

Jesus' Lonely Agony in the Garden

[Matthew 26:36-46; Mark 14:26-42; Luke 22:39-46]

When supper was over, Jesus and the eleven disciples still with him sang a hymn. They then went out together to the quiet of the Garden of Gethsemane on the Mount of Olives away from the crowds.

Jesus especially yearned for solitude. "My soul is very sorrowful even to death," he said after they had reached a quiet spot. "Wait here and watch and pray that you are not tempted to cowardice."

Jesus himself walked on about a stone's throw further into the woods and knelt down and prayed. He was in such agony of spirit that sweat came from him like drops of blood.

"Father," he prayed, "if it be possible, save me from this death. However, let not my will but your will be done." When at last Jesus saw clearly God's will for him, angels came and comforted him.

Jesus was surprised and disappointed when he returned to his disciples, for he found they had all gone to sleep. After a while he woke them, saying, "Arise. Let us now be going. The one who is to betray me is near at hand."

The Trial before the Priests

[Matthew 26:57-68; Mark 14:53-65; John 18:12-24]

Even as he was speaking a crowd of men with swords and clubs appeared in the garden. At their head was Judas. He ran up to Jesus as if happy to see him, and gave him a kiss; immediately the armed men seized Jesus and led him bound back to the temple and to the court of the high priest. Seventy priestly judges were already there in the judgment hall, sitting around an open fire.

Witnesses were also on hand, prepared to make charges against Jesus. Some said things that were not at all true; others reported rumors based on careless hearsay, and they contradicted one another.

Finally the high priest himself turned to Jesus and asked, "What answer have you to make to these charges against you?" But Jesus was silent. He said not a word.

The high priest spoke again. "Give me a true 'yes' or 'no' answer. Are you or are you not the Messiah of the Jews, whom they call the Son of God?"

"Why do you ask me?" said Jesus. "I have been doing nothing in secret. I have been teaching in synagogues and in the temple where all the Jews gather together. Ask those who have heard me, what I have said. But if you do not understand now, some day you shall know, for the time will come when you shall see the Son of Man sitting at God's right hand on a cloud in heaven and coming down to set up God's kingdom on the earth."

"Blasphemy!" shouted the high priest. "What further need have we for witnesses?" And all the other priests agreed, saying, "He is worthy of death."

The court then turned into a senseless rabble. They blindfolded Jesus, spit upon him, hit him blow upon blow with the palms of their hands. They jeered at him, called, "Now prophesy to us!"

The Trial before Pilate

[Matthew 27:1-31; Mark 15:1-20; Luke 23:1-25; John 18:28-40; 19:1-16]

The next morning Jesus was bound and led to the judgment hall of Pilate, the Roman governor. A large and excited crowd gathered in an open courtyard outside.

"What is the accusation you make against this man?" asked Pilate of the priests.

"We have a law and by that law he ought to die, because he has named himself the Son of God. If you release this man, you are not Caesar's friend, for whoever makes himself king sets himself against Caesar."

Pilate then asked Jesus, "Are you the King of the Jews? Is this what you have been teaching?"

Jesus answered, "My kingdom is not of this world; if my kingdom were of this world, then would my servants fight, that I should not be delivered to the Jews."

"So you are a king?" said Pilate.

"You say so," said Jesus. "For this I was born and for this I have come into the world, to bear witness to the truth. Everyone who is of the truth listens to me."

"What is truth?" asked Pilate. But he did not wait for Jesus' answer. He walked out into the open court where an hysterical crowd was waiting. "I find no crime against this man," Pilate said to them. "But you have a custom that I should release one prisoner each year at the time of the Passover. Would you prefer Barabbas, the robber, or this Jesus whom you say calls himself King of the Jews?"

The crowd's wild answer echoed over and over through the open court. "Release Barabbas. Crucify Jesus!"

Pilate tried several times to persuade the priests and the crowd to let him merely flog Jesus and then free him, for, he said, "I find no fault in him." Finally Pilate realized that he was gaining nothing and that a riot was beginning. So he called for a basin of water, and before all the crowd he washed his hands, saying, "I am innocent of this man's blood; see to it yourselves." At that the people cried, "His blood be on us and on our children!"

The soldiers then led Jesus back into Pilate's palace. First he was flogged. Then they stripped off his clothes, put a purple robe on him, made a crown of thorns and placed it on his head, and put a scepter in his right hand. They then began to mock him, kneeling

"Father, forgive them, for they know not what they do."

Note the many symbols around the picture — the whips, the pelican giving her blood for her young, the violet for loyalty, the butterfly for immortality, the crown of thorns, the nails, the spear, and the sponge.

down before him, slapping his face and crying out, "Hail, King of the Jews!" They spit on him and struck him with the scepter.

The Son of God Is Sacrificed

[Matthew 27:32-56; Mark 15:21-39; Luke 23:26-49; John 19:17-30]

After enduring these tortures, Jesus was given back his clothes. Soldiers led him away to the barren hillock called Golgotha where criminals were commonly crucified. Along the way a curious and excited mob gathered and followed the procession—some shouting their curses, others weeping as if their hearts would break.

Soon three crosses stood against the sky on the dreary hillside. On them hung three tortured men—two robbers and, between them, the Son of God. On a board above his head, in large letters, glared the words, "This is the King of the Jews!" Although the day was but half gone by, darkness at once spread over all the land.

Those who passed by derided Jesus, shaking their heads, saying, "If you are the Son of God, come down from the cross!" The leaders of the Jews also mocked him, saying, "He saved others, himself he cannot save. He trusts in God. Let God deliver him now, and we will believe him."

But Jesus answered not a word. He knew that it was God's plan that he should suffer and give his life, a perfect sacrifice, for the life of the world. In spite of the burning pains and in spite of the sneering hateful mob, he could pray, "Father, forgive them, for they know not what they do."

When at last his body could endure no longer, he yielded up his spirit in death. Immediately an earthquake shook the city and all the country around. Rocks were split apart. The curtain in the holy of holies in the temple was torn from top to bottom. Even graves were opened and many who had fallen asleep in death were raised to life again. Those who witnessed these wonders exclaimed, "Surely this was the Son of God!"

God Restores His Son to Life

[Matthew 28:1-15; Mark 16:1-13; Luke 24:1-49; John 20:1-31; 21:1-23]

On the morning of the third day after Jesus died and was buried, some women friends came to the tomb to perfume his body and to prepare it for a permanent burial. When they arrived, however, they found to their great surprise that the stone that closed the tomb had already been rolled away from the door. They entered, expecting to find the body of their Lord; instead they saw an angel sitting on the slab of stone. His garments were white as snow and dazzling as lightning. The women bowed their faces to the ground in fear.

"Be not afraid," said the angel kindly. "You came to find Jesus, but he is not here. He has risen from the dead as he told you he would do. Go and tell his disciples."

Trembling with fear, but at the same time wildly happy, the women fled from the tomb. But before they had gotten out of the garden, Jesus himself met them and greeted them. "Hail, my friends." When they realized it was truly their Lord, they kneeled down and worshiped him, touching his feet with their hands.

During the weeks that followed, Jesus appeared unexpectedly for a few moments in one place after another to a few special people, and then disappeared. At one time a number of his followers were gathered in a room whose doors were all tightly closed. Suddenly Jesus stood among them, although no door had been opened. At another time he suddenly joined two old friends as they were walking together through the country. Jesus began talking to them about the prophets and God's plan for the salvation of the world. Then he disappeared as suddenly as he had appeared. The men realized after he was gone that it had been their Lord. At another time, seven of Jesus' fishermen friends had spent the night in a boat on the Sea of Galilee, but had failed to catch any fish.

In the grey light of early dawn, they were surprised to see Jesus standing on the shore. He called to them to cast their nets again. This they did with remarkable success. Later they sat together on the sandy shore eating the fish they had broiled, while Jesus talked with them.

The Son of God Is Taken Back To Heaven
[Matthew 28:16-20; Mark 16:19-20; Acts 1:1-11]

At the end of forty days, Jesus made an appointment to meet his eleven loyal disciples on a certain mountaintop. When he appeared they bowed to the ground before him in worship.

"Lord, is this the time now when you will usher in the kingdom of God?" they asked earnestly.

"It is not for you to know the time of the coming of the kingdom of God. Wait in Jerusalem until you have received the power that only the Holy Spirit can give. Then go, and make disciples of all nations, baptizing them in the name of the Father and of the Son and of the Holy Spirit, teaching them to observe all that I have commanded you; and, lo, I am with you always, even unto the end of the world."

When Jesus had said these words, and while the disciples were looking on, he was lifted up and a cloud took him out of their sight.

As they were gazing upward in wonder and amazement, two men in white robes stood by them, and said, "Men of Galilee, why do you stand gazing up into heaven? This Jesus who was taken from you into heaven will come back sometime in the same way you have seen him go."

When the vision had faded away, these eleven followers of Jesus returned to Jerusalem. Hope and faith had cast out their fear and despair. Had they not been witnesses of the greatest events in history? Had they not talked and eaten and slept with the Son of God? Had they not suffered with him as he gave his life as a

While the disciples were looking on, he was lifted up and a cloud received him out of their sight.

ransom for the sins of the world? Had they not seen him alive after his death? Had they not witnessed his return to heaven? Was he not even then sitting at God's right hand? Surely it was true, as Jesus had said, "All power has been given me in heaven and on the earth." And was not the best still to come when once more God's only Son would come again in glory and power, and every knee would bow in homage to him and every tongue would "confess that Jesus Christ is Lord, to the glory of God the Father"?

So the Sixth Great Age of Time ended in the hope of a glorious second coming of the Son of God.

The Seventh Great Age of Time

Baptism With the Fire Of the Holy Spirit
[Acts 2:1-47; 4:4]

It was fifty days after the Passover. The feast of Pentecost was being observed in Jerusalem. A few of Jesus' faithful disciples had gathered in an upper room where they were talking together of the things that had happened.

Suddenly they heard the roar of a strong wind blowing violently through the room. Flashes of fire were bursting all around. These turned into what were like tongues of fire that distributed themselves so that one rested on each head. The promise Jesus had given had come true. Each one had been baptized with the fire of the Holy Spirit.

To their surprise they found they could speak as never before, and in languages they had not studied. When they left the room and walked around among the crowds of foreigners who were in Jerusalem to celebrate the festival, they discovered they could speak and understand their many languages.

This was amazing to every one. "What does this mean?" people were asking. Some mocked the disciples, saying, "They are merely drunk with wine." But the disciples themselves believed that the Spirit of God had come upon them and that greater wonders would soon be performed. Perhaps the end of the world was near at hand, when the sun would be turned into darkness and the moon into blood, and the Lord Jesus Christ would come again.

When Peter explained this meaning to people, they asked him, "What shall we do?" He answered, "Repent, and be baptized, every one of you, in the name of Jesus Christ for the forgiveness of your sins; and you too shall receive the gift of the Holy Spirit. The promise is to all." There were added that day about three thousand persons to the number baptized.

From that day on, the disciples realized more fully than before why Jesus had been crucified. They believed that he who had lived with them day by day, who had often been hungry and thirsty, had really been God himself, the creator of all animals and plants and all the oceans. They believed that he who had been poor, with no home of his own where he might rest, had really been the one to whom belonged all the riches of the earth. They believed that he who had suffered the disgrace and the torture of death on a cross was really he who could release men from all pain and raise the dead to life.

The disciples could not keep the good news to themselves. They went from house to house and from town to town, telling the good news of Jesus' death and resurrection. They said, "The Messiah—the King for whom we have been hoping—has already been here, but he was not recognized. In ignorance, our rulers crucified him. But God has used the wrath of men to praise him. Jesus submitted to this punishment voluntarily in order that he might be the perfect sacrifice—the divine Lamb of God—who by his death could save others from the need to die."

Those who believed proclaimed this good news—this gospel —wherever they went. They were sure they had the proof that this Jesus was truly the Son of God. Many declared they had seen him alive after he had been killed. "Let every one repent, therefore, and accept this wonderful forgiveness and be baptized." Before long there were five thousand numbered among the saved.

Both Honored and Persecuted

[Acts 3:1-11; 5:12-16; 12:1-19]

As the disciples began preaching this gospel to the people, they were given the power to do miraculous things, such as Jesus himself had done. Peter especially did a great deal of healing of the sick and casting out of devils. His power became so famous that people used to carry the sick on couches and lay them down by the roadside so that, as Peter walked by, his shadow might fall on them and heal them.

Others, however, were offended by these worshipers of a crucified Lord, risen from the dead. To many Jews it was a stumbling block to believing the gospel, to think of the Messiah, the Son of the Most High, being crucified as a criminal. The priests in the temple did not like the way Peter and the other disciples criticized the Jewish leaders for what they had done to Jesus, and they were irritated by the way these enthusiasts for a crucified Lord excited the crowds by healing the sick and casting out devils.

Peter and his companions were arrested in the temple while preaching and were taken before the court of the priests, where they were accused of disturbing the peace. They were commanded never to preach again in public and, after being flogged, were freed. But the followers of the Savior God were unwilling to obey the Jewish rulers when they thought God commanded them to speak. When again they appeared in the temple, and crowds were praising them and seeking to be healed, the disciples were put in jail. But they were freed by an angel who entered the jail during the night and opened the door.

Because of the growing antagonism of the men in power, some of the followers of the Savior fled from Palestine and found refuge in foreign lands. All these persecutions, however, merely added to the strength of the new society that was growing by leaps and bounds. By being scattered far and wide in different countries, the disciples were given larger opportunities to spread the news of the gospel, and they became even more earnest in their preaching.

Saul, A Persecutor, Becomes Paul, An Apostle

[Acts 6:8-15; chap. 7, 8, 9:1-31; 22:6-21; 26:12-23; I Corinthians 15:20-22; Ephesians 3:7-19; Philippians 2:5-11]

One of the most fanatic of the persecutors of these followers of Jesus was Saul, a Jewish student living in the Greek city of Tarsus to the north of Palestine. He had come down to Jerusalem to study with the rabbis, and had become a violent leader in the fight against the Jesus enthusiasts. They were being arrested and tried by the score. Some were imprisoned and others were even stoned.

One of the most notable of these Jesus enthusiasts was Stephen. Saul was active in finding false witnesses against Stephen at his trial, and he led in the final stoning. But it seems Saul was later troubled by this experience, though he tried to forget it. But he could not forget Stephen's defense of himself and the look on his face as he was about to die, and the way he prayed even while in agony that God would not hold this stoning against his persecutors. Yet Saul continued to harangue against these Jesus enthusiasts and to clamor for their death.

Not long after this, Saul, still breathing out the spirit of hate, went to the high priest in Jerusalem and asked for the names of the followers of this Jesus Christ who were in the synagogues of Damascus. Saul was on his way there, intending to arrest them and bring them bound to Jerusalem to be tried and punished.

Suddenly, at midday, a bright light from heaven flashed about Saul, and he fell blinded to the ground. As he lay helpless, he heard a voice saying, "Saul, Saul, why do you persecute me?"

Suddenly, at midday, a bright light from heaven flashed about Saul, and he fell blinded to the ground.

"Who are you, Lord?" asked Saul.

"I am Jesus whom you are persecuting."

"What shall I do, Lord?"

"Rise and stand on your feet," said the voice, "for I have appeared to you for the purpose of sending you to open men's eyes that they may turn from darkness to light and from the power of the devil to God, that they may be given forgiveness of sins and a place in heaven among those who have faith in me."

Obedient to this heavenly vision, Saul and his companions continued on their way to Damascus. For three days Saul was blind, but he spent the hours in fasting and praying, and a great change came over him. When Ananias, one of the followers of the risen Christ, came to see him and talk with him, Saul was ready to be baptized. At the very earliest opportunity he attended a synagogue service and openly declared his change of mind and heart. From that day on he was called Paul instead of Saul. The man who had been the most violent of the persecutors became the most influential of all the early preachers of the gospel.

Paul had unbounded courage. Tirelessly he made his way from city to city preaching Christ—the crucified and risen Son of God. He traveled in all the countries bordering the northeastern shore of the Mediterranean Sea. He preached in synagogues and in market places, in private homes and in the judgment halls of emperors. As these groups grew, they were organized into churches and they were given the name of Christians, meaning worshipers of Jesus the Christ, the Son of God, the Savior of the world.

In his journeyings Paul was often exposed to cold and dangers from wild animals. Again and again he was arrested and brought to trial, both in Jewish courts and in the courts of Roman governors. Many times he was flogged and imprisoned. Three times he was shipwrecked and once he was left adrift a night and a day at sea. Once he was even stoned. Finally he pleaded his cause before Caesar in Rome, where it is supposed he was either given to the lions or beheaded. But all the hardships Paul endured were to him as nothing compared with the "unsearchable riches" that had come to him through Christ.

His one unquenchable ambition was this: to help men to understand and to accept the "eternal purpose" which God had accomplished through Jesus Christ, his Son. He wanted all people of all races and lands and tongues to know that he who had been equal with God in heaven had taken upon himself the likeness of a man, and had humbled himself unto death—even the shameful death on a cross. "Therefore, God has highly exalted him," said Paul. "He has bestowed upon him a name that is above every name, that at the name of Jesus every knee should bow and every tongue confess that Jesus Christ is Lord, to the glory of God the Father. As in the beginning death came because of Adam's sin, so now eternal life has come because of Christ. As in Adam all die, even so in Christ shall all be made alive.

"Such a glorious hope is now ours," he said, "not because we have earned the right to eternal happiness. It is all due to the love of God, that has been shown us in Christ Jesus. Anyone who has the faith to accept this Savior is secure in God's good pleasure and is assured of eternal bliss. But anyone who refuses to accept him is the object of God's just wrath against sinners through all eternity."

Paul added other important teachings. Those who accept Jesus as Savior should also accept and develop within themselves the same kind of spirit that Jesus had when he lived on the earth. As Jesus had set his mind on things above, and not on things on the earth, his followers should do the same. "Put to death, therefore, what is earthly in you; all immorality, evil desire, anger, malice, slander, foul talk, and lying. Instead, put on a new nature, having compassion, kindness, lowliness, meekness, patience, forgiving one another. Above all these put on love."

God's Plan of Salvation Still Unfinished

[Revelation 1:1-3]

The promise given by the angel at the time Jesus was lifted up to heaven was never forgotten by Jesus' followers. Although no one claimed to know just when Christ would come, yet every one believed it would not be long. The hope of his second coming often filled the minds of the early Christians. What would it be like on the day of his coming? they wondered. Would they recognize him sitting on a throne at the right hand of God? Some had fantastic visions of this great day of the Lord.

To one disciple, named John, who was living in seclusion on the Island of Patmos, was given a series of visions. God commanded him to write down what he saw in his visions, and to have them preserved in a book (it is called *Revelation*) so that all men might know what to expect when God finally fully completes his great plan for the eternal destiny of mankind.

Although these first Christians waited in almost daily expectation of the second coming of Christ, yet weeks, months, years, and even centuries went by and still there was no sign of his return. Instead there were wars here and wars there. False leaders arose who stirred up the people's hopes, only to leave them disillusioned. Thousands of Christians were persecuted. Some were imprisoned and others were thrown into cages with lions. Yet the courage of these Christians was undaunted. They died believing they were entering into the glory of heaven, to live with Christ for ever more.

During the many centuries since that day, again and again men have expected Christ to come soon—yet he still has not come. There is an unfinished part to God's plan of salvation which is still to be in the future. The revelation shown by God to John tells of the end, and adds confirmation to the words of the prophets of Israel.

The Devil will be chained and dropped into the bottomless pit.

A Thousand Years of Peace

[Matthew 24:3-14; Revelation 19:11-21; 20:1-15]

Before the great day of Christ's coming, there will be great suffering on the earth. "Nation will rise up against nation, and kingdom against kingdom, and there will be famines and earthquakes in various places; all this will be but the beginning of the sufferings. . . . False prophets will arise, and lead many astray. Because wickedness will be multiplied, most men's love will grow cold"; but not till the gospel is preached throughout the whole world, as a testimony to all nations, will the end come.

On the day of his coming, the sky will be opened, and one sitting on a white horse will come down to earth. His eyes will be like flames of fire and in his mouth he will carry a sharp sword and in his hand will be a scepter of iron with which he will rule the nations. His white robe will be stained with blood, and on it will be written the words "King of kings and Lord of lords." And behind the conquering one will come the soldiers of the armies of heaven, also on white horses.

In the meantime the armies of the devil—with all the kings of wickedness—will array themselves against the armies of heaven and they will fight a fierce battle in a place called Armageddon. The King of kings will defeat them. Many will be slain, while others will be thrown alive into the lake of fire. And the devil himself will be captured and chained and dropped into the bottomless pit underneath the earth, and the door locked above him.

Then Christ will set up his throne in Jerusalem, and the kings of all the world will bow before him. The age-old dream of the Hebrew people will come true. The kingdom of God will be established in Zion, with the Savior of all the world on the throne. And he will rule the nations with justice, and there will be peace in all lands for a thousand years.

The Final Day of Judgment

[Revelation 1:8; 5:12; 6:12-14; 19:6; 20:11-15; 21:8; 1 Corinthians 15:51-53]

Suddenly at a time known only to God, the sun will be darkened and the moon become blood. The stars in the sky will fall as the fig tree sheds its winter fruit when shaken by a gale; the sky will vanish like a scroll that is rolled up and the earth will be melted in fire.

When the first heaven and the first earth have passed away, a new heaven and a new earth will be created. And the holy city, the new Jerusalem, will come down out of heaven from God, and a great voice from the throne will cry, "Behold, the dwelling of God is with men. He will dwell with them, and they shall be his people."

The radiance of the holy city will be like that of many rare jewels. Its walls will be of jasper and its streets pure gold. There will be no temple there, for God himself and the divine Lamb are greater than any temple. There will be no need for a sun or moon, for the glory of God will be its light. The gates of the city will never be shut, for there will be no night there.

At the sound of a heavenly trumpet, all the dead will be raised. In a moment, in the twinkling of an eye, their perishable nature will be changed and they will put on bodies that can never be corrupted or die. Then those who are still alive on the earth and those who have been raised from the dead will all gather before the throne of God and before his Son, who will be seated at God's right hand.

The great book of life will then be opened, in which are written the names of all those who, during their lifetime, repented of their wrong-doing, accepted Christ as Savior, and were baptized.

Those before the throne whose names are written in this book of life will be permitted to enter the city of God where they may live with Christ in perfect happiness forever and ever. God shall wipe away every tear from their eyes. Death shall be no more; neither shall there be mourning, nor crying, nor pain any more.

The multitude of the saved will come from every nation and tongue and people on the earth. Their number will be ten thousand times ten thousand, and thousands of thousands. The sound of their song will be like the sound of many waters and like many thunder peals.

"Hallelujah! for the Lord our God, the Almighty, reigns!"

"To him who sits upon the throne and to the Lamb be blessing and honor and glory and power forever and ever!"

Their peace and joy will surpass all our understanding.

But those whose names are not written in the book of life will be cast into the lake of fire, with the devil, where they shall suffer torment in its burning flames forever and ever. For the cowardly, the faithless, the polluted, murderers, sexual sinners, sorcerers, idolators, and liars cannot inherit the kingdom of heaven unless their sins have been washed away with the blood of Christ.

Between heaven and hell there will be a great gulf fixed so that those who might repent in hell and wish to pass over into heaven can never do so. "The judgments of the Lord are true and righteous altogether." They cannot be changed. The Savior God is "the first and the last, the beginning and the end, the Lord God who is and was and who is to come, the Almighty."

In this manner the Seventh Great Age of Time will come to an end, and for all humanity eternity will begin. Mankind will be divided forever into two communities—one living forever in perfect harmony and bliss with God, the other condemned to everlasting torture.

The Day of Judgment — The Final Division of Mankind

PART TWO

THE UNANSWERED QUESTION:
"WHAT IS TRUTH?"

Accept no person against thine own soul,
And let no reverence for any man cause thee to fall.
But let the counsel of thine own heart stand:
For there is none more faithful unto thee than it.
For a man's mind is sometime wont to bring him tidings,
More than seven watchmen, that sit above in a high tower.

ECCLESIASTICUS[2]

Questions the Story Raises

Now that you have read this Old Story of Salvation through to the end, your feelings about it may be mixed, even contradictory. You may be profoundly moved by the grandeur and pathos of this tremendous drama. Perhaps it has brought back memories of early childhood, or has reminded you of parents, grandparents, uncles, aunts, friends, whose daily lives are still guided by unquestioning belief in this Old Story of Salvation. On the one hand, you may be wishing that you too could believe it all. On the other hand, you may be hoping to find a way to prove that it cannot all be true.

Whatever your feelings may be, there are probably ideas in the story that you feel need to be clarified. Is this truly the Christian gospel? Is it the "good news" that Jesus himself had to tell? How may a person decide? Does this story express your philosophy of life? Can you accept and believe it? How different is your faith from "the faith of our fathers"?

We hope that readers, whether young people or adults, can meet together after reading this story in order to talk over all these matters frankly and carefully. This Old Story of Salvation needs to be lived with, over and over, in order to be appreciated or even to be justly criticized. We need to be conscious of its presence as an undergirding framework within which our Western culture has grown. We need to find it and to understand it in our history, our literature, our art, our music and song. We need personally to feel its power imaginatively in our own attempts to paint it, to sing it, to dramatize it, or to dance it.

This second part of the book, therefore, suggests ways for

groups to think over the story together, to bring questions and feelings out into the open for discussion. Some of the questions other readers have raised are listed here. We have attempted to discuss these, not for the purpose of pointing to the correct answers, but with the thought of bringing into focus the most pertinent facts and issues that need to be considered before answering. The author's own point of view may be apparent at times. We beg, however, that no thought be given your allegiance until it becomes thoroughly at home in your own mind.

1. The Bible as the Source of the Story of Salvation

Is this the story that the Bible tells?

How much of it is history and how much of it is legend or the way people long ago believed about things?

Is this "the story of the Bible," as some people say? The answer is both "yes" and "no." It is the story the Bible tells if one thinks of the Bible in the old way, as "the Holy Book" in which God has revealed his plan of salvation or his story of man's history, destiny, and hope. It is the story that millions of people *have thought* and millions *still think* the Bible tells.

It is not the story the Bible tells for those who search this collection of sixty-six ancient books, as they would search the writings of other men, to find out what may have been the historical experiences behind the records. It is not the story the Bible tells for those who study it in order to find the words of men, rather than "the word of God."[3]

It is, however, a story that *has come out of the Bible*. In fact, it has come out of two Bibles now joined into one. The first of these was the Jewish Bible, which is the one Jesus studied in the synagogue. Christians now call this the *Old Testament,* meaning the *Old Covenant with God,* or *God's Old Plan of Salvation.*

After Jesus had lived and died, many people came to believe that he had risen from the dead and was waiting in heaven, expecting to return to the earth in glory as the Messiah or Christ, the Savior of the world. His followers believed that the greatest events in all history had come to pass when Jesus was crucified and rose from the dead. The tragedy of the cross became for them the glorious sign of God's boundless love for all mankind.

Peter and Paul, the first two great preachers of the gospel of this risen Christ, saw in all these happenings and in the promise of Christ's second coming the fulfillment of the history recorded in the *Old Testament*. Some among them began to feel the need to get accounts of these stupendous happenings written down. During the latter part of the first century and on into the second century, these ardent believers in the Savior God began collecting everything that had been written about him and all they could find that told of the beginnings of this new sect called Christian. Finally, sometime in the fourth century after Christ, a committee chose twenty-seven of these documents which they judged to be the best. These were gathered together in one book and given the name *New Testament*, or the *New Covenant*, or *God's New Plan of Salvation*.

Among the books chosen was that remarkable one called *Revelation*, which is the record of a vision had by one of the persecuted Christians, exiled on the Island of Patmos. He was not the John who was one of the twelve disciples of Jesus, but a now unknown character, living sometime during the second century. With John's vision of the catastrophic destruction of the material universe, the resurrection of all the world's dead, and the final separation of mankind on the Day of Judgment into heaven and hell, the Story of Salvation was extended into eternity.

Although Paul had conceived the main outline of this Story of Salvation—its basic ideas were the substance of his preaching— yet the full story was not gathered together in writing in the dramatic form of the *Seven Great Ages of Time* until St. Augustine, the giant intellect among the Christian leaders of the early fifth century, set it forth.

This then, put very briefly, is how this Story of Salvation grew out of the two Bibles, now combined in one. The first Christians saw the life, death, resurrection, and second coming of the Christ in the background of the history they knew and of the early Hebrew tales of the creation and fall of man. We might say, on the one hand, that this Story of Salvation grew out of the old Jewish Bible; and, on the other hand, we might also say that the Jewish-Christian Bible grew out of belief in the Story of Salvation.

But knowing and understanding this Story of Salvation is not the same as knowing and understanding the Jewish-Christian Bible.

For one thing, the Story of Salvation, as told here, is much shorter than the sixty-six books in the Old and New Testaments. The story includes only those parts of the Bible that are in narrative form, whereas almost half of the Old Testament is sermons, laws, proverbs, hymns, descriptions of ceremonies, and lists of genealogies. And all but six of the New Testament books are personal letters written either to the churches or to individuals. The Story of Salvation omits all these less dramatic books. Some of the episodes related are considerably shortened; a few personalities of importance have scarcely been mentioned, and some have even been omitted entirely. Portions of the Bible which to many students seem to be the most sublime expressions of aspiration, such as some of the Psalms and the stirring sermons of the great prophets of Israel, have been omitted. So knowing the Story of Salvation is not equal to knowing the Bible.

A certain historical period, however, in the life of the people of Israel and in the development of the Christian Church is covered by both the Bible and this Story of Salvation. We can look at the important dates in this history as a kind of backdrop in front of which the drama of both moves. Since it may be convenient to refer to these basic dates occasionally, we list them here where they

can be easily seen. The period includes about twenty-two hundred years.

Migration of Abraham and his tribe into Canaan ......c. 2000 B.C.E.

Exodus of Israelites from Egypt under Moses ....c. 1250-1200 B.C.E.

Reign of Saul ....c. 1020-1004 B.C.E.

Reign of David ....c. 1004-960 B.C.E.

Division of Kingdom of Israel ....925 B.C.E.

Destruction of Samaria ....722 B.C.E.

Destruction of Jerusalem ....586 B.C.E.

Return of exiles to Jerusalem under Ezra ....458 B.C.E.

Birth of Jesus (traditional date) ....Year 0

Crucifixion of Jesus ....c. 30 A.D.

Peter's martyrdom ....c. 64 A.D.

Paul's martyrdom ....c. 67 A.D.

Final destruction of Jerusalem by Romans ....70 A.D.

The writing of the earliest gospel ....c. 70 A.D.

The writing of *Luke* ....c. 100 A.D.

The writing of *John* ....c. 120 A.D.

The writing of *Revelation* ....c. 120 A.D.

"B.C.E." means "Before the Common Era." In Christian tradition, the usual
letters used are "B.C.," meaning "Before Christ." We prefer the form on which
Christians and Jews can unite.

The letter "c." stands for the Latin word *"circa,"* meaning "around" or
"about."

This then is the historical frame within which both the Jewish-
Christian Bible and *The Old Story of Salvation* move. Abraham,
Isaac, Jacob, Moses, David, Solomon, Ahab, Elijah, Jesus, Peter,
and Paul were all real persons who once lived. *The Old Story of
Salvation* is the same as the Bible, in that it gives the main episodes
told in its narrative portions. It is, in a sense, a simplified Bible.
But it is the Bible story presented from a biased point of view
—namely, that of the early Christian Church. It presents the

traditional Christian interpretation of the Hebrew scriptures, to which the Christian Church added its philosophy about the significance of Jesus' life and death and its understanding of the importance of the beginnings of the Christian Church.

To the unbiased student of today, however, the Bible is not a book that reveals the truth about God, presenting with assurance what he hoped for, planned, and did to save mankind from the punishment due him for his sins. It is instead a book about people and what they hoped for, planned, and did in the light of their beliefs about God. Nor does the Bible, as seen by scholars, reveal what God has clearly commanded and condemned, but rather what the men who produced the Bible thought about right and wrong in the light of their beliefs about both God and man.[4]

This Old Story of Salvation is a time-honored and powerful tradition. It is a dramatic summation of the great beliefs about God, the universe, life and death, that the Christian Church has for centuries regarded as the Christian faith. From time to time, some of these beliefs have been revised; some have even been rather generally abandoned. Different Protestant sects have been responsible for their own kinds of revision.

But the Old Story of Salvation, as given in this book, is the root out of which all variations have developed. It may be called the original Christian faith—*not, however, what Jesus himself believed, but what the Christian Church early came to believe about Jesus.* In studying this old story, we are studying not history directly, but rather a great tradition that has molded history and that is still greatly influencing men's attitudes and convictions.

The Holy Spirit — The Third Person of the Christian Trinity

The shining disk in the original is of gold. The angels suggest heaven.

2. Creation and Evolution

Can a person believe the story of creation as it is in the Bible
and believe in evolution too?

Is the story of Adam and Eve a myth?

Can a myth be true?

Anyone already familiar with the first two chapters of Genesis knows that the Bible contains two different stories of the
beginnings of the universe and man, one in the first chapter and
another in the second. In these two accounts, both the order of
creation and the method are different. It is, therefore, quite impossible to accept both as being literally true.

Those who have read other stories of beginnings,[5] handed
down traditionally in other countries and among other peoples
beside the Hebrews, will appreciate how all such stories of beginnings grew out of men's imaginations. Since no thinking human
being was alive to observe creation, it is impossible for any one to
make positive assertions. The scientists have, however, learned
how to read the rocks and the stars, and they are convinced from
the evidences they have found that it has taken aeons of time to
bring the universe to its present stage. Consequently the Biblical
accounts of creation are today quite widely regarded as poetry,
allegory, or myth.

It is important, however, to realize that this sentiment is one
which has been desperately resisted by the Christian Church. The
theory of evolution, proposed in 1859 by Charles Darwin, was
fought for decades, some American states even forbidding the
teaching of evolution in the public schools.

The reason for this strong resistance to belief in evolution lies
in the importance of the story of creation to the entire Story of
Salvation. To explain the first chapter of Genesis by saying that
the days of creation were not the short days which we know now,

but poetic ways of expressing the passing of long periods of time, was not too difficult. But even this involved a radical change in thought when the idea was first proposed, because for many years English Christian Bibles (the King James version) commonly contained a line above the first chapter of Genesis giving the date of creation as having been in 4004 B.C. Dr. John Lightfoot, Vice Chancellor of Cambridge University in the seventeenth century, declared that, after having made exhaustive calculations, he was convinced that man was created on October 23, at nine o'clock in the morning, in the year 4004 B.C.[6]

Orthodox Jewish scholars for some reason set the date of creation two hundred and forty-four years later than this Christian date. On the cornerstone of the Jewish Theological Seminary in New York City two dates are given, 1929 and 5689, the second date being the number of years since the creation of man. Both of these illustrations are startling examples of how long ancient ideas once established in a culture can endure.

Another reason that the idea of the mythical character of the Adam and Eve story has been resisted so long is that it presents the problem that gives the motive for the entire Story of Salvation. "In Adam's fall we sinned all," said the old New England primer. That tragic initial event when the first man and woman disobeyed God and thus corrupted their very natures is the cornerstone on which the entire Story of Salvation was built. If man had not fallen, he would not have needed a divine Savior.

Many theologians, therefore, now say that there are truths in the myth of Adam and Eve, and they are these: Man originally was made sinless by a perfect God. In the beginning man's relationship to God was happy and satisfying. But the first man and woman broke that relationship. They became estranged from God because of their disobedience. This is man's great tragedy. He lost his favor with God and his feeling of harmony with him. Ever since that time man has been seeking to recover his loss. But his nature has become too corrupt to enable him to regain his "salvation" by his own will power or his own efforts. He has to depend on God's special help (God's grace, as it is called). Man needs a divine Savior.

This way of interpreting the Adam and Eve story is being presented rather commonly at the present time. This will be discussed further under the topic "Human Nature and Sin."

Returning to the first and second chapters of Genesis, let us examine some of the contrasts between ideas in the Bible version of creation and ideas vital to the theory of evolution. Can one believe both?

First of all, in the Biblical stories, all the acts of creation were completed at a certain definite time. For the evolutionist, the new is continually emerging. New stars appear; new planets are being formed. When once a species has emerged and for a time resisted life's hazards successfully, there seems to be a long time lag before a new species emerges. Nevertheless, the evolutionist expects the new to appear, and the scientific experimenter is even participating in the processes that lead toward new "creations." To the modern evolutionist, creation is continuous.

Again, in the Biblical narratives, the power to create belongs to God alone. God is a perfect, all-powerful divine being who is wholly other than humanity and who lives above and beyond the natural universe. God is both *outside the universe* in a supernatural realm, and *outside humanity* in a superhuman realm. This God has created all that is by the power of his thought and will.

According to the evolutionist of today, the power to "create" the new is *within* the very nature of all living things themselves. The whole universe seems to be alive and creative—expanding, multiplying, living, dying, and living again. (This is quite different from the theory of evolution as proposed by Darwin, who conceived of the new as emerging entirely by chance, and of the universe as a mechanism.)

To the modern evolutionist, the very word "creation" is taking on a new meaning. It is a process of *emerging out of* or of *being born from* something already alive, rather than a process of being "made" by a "Creator" who is wholly other than the thing created.

Most scientists today, however, would not feel justified in asserting with certainty that no Creative Divinity exists outside the universe. They merely accept with humility their inability to explore beyond the bounds of the natural. Nor does the scientist attempt to say how everything began. Indeed, he does not yet see evidence that there ever was a beginning. The natural universe seems eternal. It looks as though we need not go to heaven to live in eternity.

This new way of conceiving of creation indicates a very great change in man's thoughts of creation and God. It has resulted in turning attention away from myth-making about what was before the world was and what is to come in the far distant future after the world ends (if it does ever end), and has led man to concentrate his powers on discovering what is around him now and what may be possible for him in the near future. We might say that much of what men used to call "supernatural," scientists are finding in the "natural," and what men used to worship as "superhuman" may really be "human."

Again, according to the Jewish-Christian stories of creation, world history began with a Golden Age. All animals and all nature were friendly to man. Man and woman were sinless and immortal. They had been made in the image of God, and God called everything that he had created "good." But when the first pair disobeyed God's command and ate of the fruit of the Tree of Knowledge of Good and Evil, they lost their purity of heart, and their immortality. They were punished with hard work, pain, sickness and death, and they felt cut off from God's favor and under his condemnation. The story of Adam and Eve, whether myth or fact, presents the first man and woman on a pinnacle of happiness, from which they fall down into the depths of despair.

The scientist has found no evidence of any such Golden Age in the beginning. In fact, all the fossils found in rocks and all the bones and implements unearthed in primitive man's first cave dwellings point in the opposite direction. Apparently the first human beings were apelike. It required millions of years for even the first savage, crude specimens of humanity to evolve. Slowly and unsteadily, the human species has been developing mental abilities, the power of speech, and those arts and crafts of civilization which have led to its superiority over other animals. The evidence suggests that man was not *made* superior in the beginning, but that he has *achieved* his superiority through ages of struggle.

Furthermore, according to the story in Genesis, sickness, labor, pain and death would never have been man's lot had he not sinned and invoked God's punishment. According to today's generally accepted scientific attitude toward life, however, labor, in moderate measure, instead of being regarded as a disgrace, is accepted as a blessing. And have we not more reasonable ways of explaining pain, sickness and death than that they are divine punishments?

And what of man's eating of the fruits of the Tree of Knowledge of Good and Evil. What knowledge can be more important for anyone to find? Instead of condemning Eve for daring to eat, should we perhaps honor her for her courage, just as Prometheus has been honored for stealing fire from heaven?

Whether the Adam and Eve story be thought of as myth or fact, what ideas are in it? And in the light of today's understanding, do these ideas seem to us to be true or false?

3.   Miracles

"How do we know that Jesus turned those two fishes into enough to feed all those people?"

"Do you really believe that Jesus healed sick people by just speaking to them?"

"Can you prove that Jesus did these things? I know the Bible says so, but you can't say that all the Bible is true—so what?"

"Do you believe that Jesus really came back to life after he was buried? How could that be?"

These are samples of the questions about miracles some readers have raised.

The following is a stenographer's report of a classroom conversation on the subject of miracles.

ROBIN: "How come miracles don't happen today?"

MARY FRANCES: "These things don't happen nowadays to us because we don't have enough faith."

ROBIN: "I think that people nowadays are just as holy. They go to church and think of God."

ELIZABETH: "Just going to church doesn't make them good."

TEACHER: "Do you think that an age of miracles existed once?"

JUDY: "I think there were *little* miracles, and they were exaggerated."

TEACHER: "What do you mean by little miracles?"

(Judy gave an illustration of a woman, blind for eleven years, who got her sight back.)

ROBIN: "Some miracles can be explained." (He referred to the time when Jesus turned water into wine.) "The people just thought they were drinking wine."

ELIZABETH: "Some grapes may have just fallen in, or it might have been like the story of the emperor and his new clothes."

JUDY: "I think that if you have faith in yourself, God will help you and that is a miracle."

ELIZABETH: "I think that miracles are going on all around us but we don't realize it. Look at that electric bulb. It's a miracle."

In order to understand what a miracle was in Biblical days, or at the time this Old Story of Salvation was commonly believed, we must put ourselves imaginatively in the place of those who thought that all nature was controlled by angels or demons or gods much as a commander controls the movements of his armies. They believed that God needed to come into the world every so often and make a special display of his power so that mankind would not forget to obey. It was not difficult for them to think that God might command the rain to stop falling, or send an angel down to the earth to spread disease among cattle and men when his creatures did not follow his bidding. And when one of God's saints such as Elijah was in danger of starving, they could imagine God as commanding the ravens to feed him; and, of course, when looking back on the life of Jesus, whom they regarded as the greatest of all God's representatives on the earth, they could imagine his being given power to heal the sick, to make lame men walk and blind men see, and even to raise the dead.

Modern man lives in an entirely different mental atmosphere. Ours is a world of physics, chemistry, astronomy, biology. Man has learned by long experience that in the nature of things there is dependability and regularity; if certain things happen, certain consequences usually follow.

Some review, perhaps even a listing, of all the miracles described in *The Old Story of Salvation* would be well worth while. Three questions regarding each of them might be asked: What was the purpose of this miracle? Who made it happen? From our modern outlook and understanding of the nature of things, how would we explain what probably happened?

A very interesting side study can be made of the history of mankind's beliefs regarding floods, sickness, and disasters generally. Legends, regarding floods, other than the one told among the Hebrews, can be found. It is not unusual even today to hear someone speak of "providence." What is meant? Does God give special protection to those whom he loves? Even though we think of our modern generation as being scientifically minded, we cannot fail to see that many of these old ideas regarding God still prevail.

Readers will think of experiences of their own and of others they have known. What kinds of prayers are heard in times of drought? Or of epidemics? Or in times of war? Can a scientifically minded person pray? How?

All such questions will lead to the most profound and basic of all questions: Do we believe in the kind of God presented in this Old Story of Salvation? If not, in what kind of God do we believe? Or must we give up all belief in God? Let us guard against any superficial certainties.

4. Human Nature and Sin

What does all this about "sin" mean? Can't we really help being bad?

In the Biblical sense, the word "sin" has two meanings. It is some definite wrong-doing which is a transgression of the moral law. When one is conscious of having committed a *sin,* he feels guilty either in relation to another person or in relation to God, the maker of moral law. In this sense some *sins* are more serious than others.

When the word "sin" is combined with the suffix *"-ful"* to make "sinful," then we have another meaning. A *sinful nature,* as conceived in this salvation story, is an inherited nature that contains such strong compulsions to do wrong that it is impossible, without the aid of God's special "grace," to live a truly "good" life. Since according to this Old Story of Salvation every one is born with "a sinful nature," man's predicament is truly tragic. The demands of society and the demands of conscience, or (in the language of this story) God's commands, urge men to kindness, honesty, love, and self-sacrifice. On the other hand, man's sinful nature leads him toward selfishness, sexual excesses and cruelty. As a result he is continually at war within himself, and his inadequacy makes him afraid of his own destruction.

This is the doctrine of "original sin." It is because of this sinful nature that a supernatural Savior is needed. Whether or not this doctrine truly represents reality is a serious question, for if it is false, this whole story of salvation loses its original meaning.

Anyone who samples the most popular Christian theological books of today will discover that many theologians and ministers accept the doctrine of original sin—with some variations, however, in their interpretations of its meaning. Dr. Paul Tillich, for example, has written, "Because man is evil he tends to give up, to surrender himself to the pressure of anxiety."[7]

Dr. Robert McCracken, minister of the Riverside Church in New York City, has spoken in this manner: "Two world wars, with a third threatening, have brought home to us that human nature has a stubborn kink in it somewhere, a bias toward evil. . . . The thing the churches call sin is no bogey erected by theologians, no ghost imagined by minds morbid with the fear of God." Rather sin is "the factor that through the centuries has brought down in ruin one civilization after another."[8]

These brief statements are but samples of similar statements frequently made by Christian ministers.

Some psychologists and psychiatrists also give support to this general idea that human nature has within it a "demonic element," although they usually avoid the word "sin." Freud believed he found in human nature certain low, animal instincts, which are compulsive in their nature. The demands of the *libido* and the demands of conscience and of society he believed to be in continual conflict. To repress and deny the existence of these instincts merely adds to their strength. Hence, they must be accepted and some substitute outlet found by means of which they can be sublimated in constructive ways. This unending conflict Freud thought of as due to man's inborn nature and hence inescapable.[9]

In more recent years, however, other psychiatrists and students of infant and child life have been revising this understanding of human nature. Dr. Karen Horney,[10] for example, came to the conclusion that these savage and destructive desires were not due to man's inborn nature, but rather to the thwarting effects of a confused culture, and man's struggle to harmonize his desires with those of others, to preserve his own integrity and at the same time to be joined in sympathy with others; to achieve his own growth and development and at the same time give room to others for a similar growth. The instinctive drives with which we are born, Dr. Horney believed to be potentially valuable. None deserves to be called evil. They are all required if the development of the personality is to be satisfactory. It is only when the struggle to fulfill life becomes too involved, and when fear and anxiety becloud the mind, that the individual feels compelled to evil and gives way to some pseudo-solution that seems to give satisfaction temporarily. Such a point of view does not deny the reality of conflict in human experience, but it suggests the possibility of man's finding ways to resolve the conflicts.

At this point, students of infant and child life have made an extraordinary contribution during the past twenty years. The activities and emotional expressions of thousands of infants have been observed, recorded and studied. The result has been a raising of respect for the potential goodness within human nature. They have found no evidence to support the theory that any of a baby's innate desires are evil in themselves. They all seem to have high potential value. In fact the young child's primary need, beyond that of physical care, is the need to be loved. This is surely a potentially good desire, and it has been proven to be essential even to a baby's health. Indeed, it is so commonly recognized as essential that pediatricians, in prescribing for children's care, use the formula T.L.C. (tender loving care). It has been demonstrated by experiments that babies do not have a normal development without this love. When deprived of clear evidences of it for long, even though all needed physical wants are met, babies have been observed to sicken and some have even died. On the other hand, if this need for love is satisfied, the baby begins to relax. He seems able to trust his environment. He begins to have faith in life.

After he has begun to experience this happiness, the baby begins to express his own love for his mother. When he has learned to exchange love, the child feels joined to others, while at the same time he feels he is something apart from anyone else. He begins to show a desire for self-direction. To be sure, he has to prove his powers, at times, by refusing adult guidance. This, however, the psychologist does not regard as sinful. The child is experimenting, and if given a happy balance between permissiveness and loving direction, he will develop feelings of personal worth. But only when such self-respect is achieved can a child want to co-operate and have a genuine interest in others.

In short, many modern child psychologists, because of their laboratory experiences with babies and young children, have become convinced that human nature is creatively endowed with certain natural urges—*all of which are potentially valuable*. The need to be independent is fully as valuable as the need to love, and the need to rebel is as valuable as the need to please. Consequently, in dealing with young children, psychologists have developed a trust and confidence in human nature which is quite foreign to traditional Christianity.

The whole movement toward more "permissive" ways with

children and toward the granting of greater freedom of choice has grown out of this changed attitude toward human nature. It is revolutionizing our ideas of parenthood and discipline.[11]

5. Punishments and Rewards—Heaven and Hell

"Why is God punishing people all the time in the Story of Salvation?"

"There isn't really a hell, is there? Everybody ought to end up in heaven sometime, wherever that is."

"But they've got to earn getting there, haven't they?"

Again it is important to identify ourselves with the early believers in the Story of Salvation in order to understand how they came to imagine God as acting and feeling as he is portrayed in this story. The Biblical records all came out of a type of culture that was autocratic and patriarchal. The father in the household, the chieftain of the tribe, and the head of the nation—all ruled in their respective circles with an iron hand. Even the father expected absolute obedience from his children, and had the power of life and death over them. It would have been almost unthinkable in those times for men in such a culture to think of God in any other way than as a lawgiver and judge.

It is indeed only very recently that this general conception of relationships in the home and in the nation has been questioned or much changed. Even now the authoritarian pattern in home, society and government is far more prevalent than the more flexible, mutually-respecting pattern of democratic relationships. And to conceive of God as the head of a democracy rather than as king of a world-wide kingdom would be shocking to most people.

The thought of a God who rules by commands, rewards and punishments is greatly strengthened if added to it is the belief that human nature, when left to its own devices, moves compulsively toward evil. As long as it is assumed that men will be bad if permitted freedom, those in power will feel compelled to discipline, to prod and warn, to threaten with punishment, and even to compel compliance by physical force. And as long as men assume that they have this instinctive drive toward evil, they cannot believe in their own worth or power, and so this very assumption weakens them and makes them unable to save themselves.

This old pattern of culture, that of a society of kings and subjects, permeates the entire Story of Salvation with the thought of a God who commands obedience and punishes disobedience. Consequently the control is from without rather than from within, and rewards and punishments must be continually used as lures or warnings.

In all periods of history, however, there have probably been persons of unusual insight and saintliness who have recognized the reservoir of worthy possibilities in the so-called ordinary person, and who have advocated trustful relationships. Here and there, before so-called "progressive education," voices were raised in protest against motivating conduct through arbitrarily set rewards or punishments. A story is told of one such person, a Moslem maid, living during the time of the Crusades. Hearing that a group of Christian pilgrims on their way to Jerusalem were to pass by along a certain road, she met them and held up before them in her right hand a pail of water and in her left hand a pan of fire.

In surprise, the Crusaders asked her why she was doing this strange thing. She replied: "With this fire, ye Christians, I would burn your Paradise, and with this water I would quench your Hell, so that thereafter ye may no longer allow yourselves to be impelled to good deeds by hope of reward, nor be frightened from evil deeds by fear of punishment, but that ye may do the good and the noble thing because it *is* good and noble and avoid the thing that is evil and ugly and wicked because it *is* evil and ugly and wicked."

Fortunately, in spite of this emphasis on punishments and

rewards, on heaven and hell, in this Story of Salvation, millions of people have been pretty well able to overlook hell and to give little thought even to the reward of a crown in heaven after death. This Old Story of Salvation has done something for them much more valuable than to warn them of eternal destruction or to promise them eternal happiness. Although others may belittle them, despise and persecute them, they have come to believe that God loves them. They are his children. Thus their self-confidence and self-respect are lifted, even though they attribute all praise to God and speak of themselves as nothing.

On the other hand, it is well to be aware of the strong and continuing influence that the darker side of this Story of Salvation has in our society, even on those who boast of their rejection of all religion. It might surprise us if some one should make a record of the number of times the words "heaven" and "hell" are mentioned, either in jest or seriously, in the ordinary conversation of typical adults, or how often swear words growing out of this belief in hell are used in temper outbursts.

And the ideas and words bandied about among adults seep into the consciousness of children. Teachers and leaders of play groups know well how often children at play debate these ideas, sometimes also in jest, but more often seriously. Sensitive children sometimes become seriously frightened and the bolder ones are made hostile toward all religion.

Bob, at six, was invited to a birthday party where the children played school together. The girl who played teacher scolded the others and talked about God and dying, and heaven and hell. She said if they were not good or if they told lies, God would strike them dead and then they would go to hell. Although it was just a game, Bob was too young at the time to understand. He was in tears by the time his mother came to take him home; instead of saying a pleasant good-bye as he left his friend's home, he shouted, "And I don't *have* to believe in God if I don't want to!"

For Bob this was an experience he could never forget. For a long time afterwards, he refused to go to Sunday school. He was determined he would not let anybody put anything over on him again. But all of Bob's friends went to Sunday school and at last he yielded. Being fortunate in the church school he attended, Bob regained his respect for religious teachers.

Any one interested in studying the history of beliefs in heaven and hell will find it a strange and fascinating story. It is appropriate here to remind ourselves of the significant contribution the Universalists of America made to Christian thought, when, beginning with John Murray and Hosea Ballou, and later supported by other courageous men and women, they rejected the idea of eternal punishment as unworthy of a good and loving God. The story of this revolt can be found in *The Church Across the Street*.[12] Certain leading Unitarians, living when John Murray and Hosea Ballou were proclaiming this new doctrine of universal salvation, were afraid of it lest sinful man should feel no motive for being good without the threat of eternal punishment facing him.

Sometimes a person entirely outside ecclesiastical circles expresses the challenge to fresh thinking more directly than a theologian can do. Oscar Wilde, a literary genius of the nineteenth century, was poetically sensitive to the genius in the man Jesus. During his time in prison, Wilde wrote these words:

"His (Jesus') morality is all sympathy, just what morality should be. If the only thing he ever said had been, 'Her sins are forgiven her because she loved much,' it would have been worthwhile dying to have it said. His justice is all poetical justice, exactly what justice should be. The beggar goes to heaven because he has been unhappy. I cannot conceive of a better reason for his being there."[13]

Was Wilde merely sentimental, or did he put into words a true insight regarding Jesus and regarding man's needed motives for living a good life?

Let us not assume that few people really believe in hell now, or that the idea is seldom preached or assumed in Christian churches. The free literature available in the vestibule of almost any Roman Catholic Church gives startling evidence of the prevalence of the idea. The following prayer was distributed recently after the funeral service of a very fine Roman Catholic physician:

"Gentlest Heart of Jesus, ever present in the Blessed Sacrament, ever consumed with burning love for the poor captive souls in Purgatory, have mercy on the soul of our departed servant.

"Be not severe in thy judgment but let some drops of Thy Precious Blood fall upon the devouring flames, and do Thou, O merciful Saviour, send Thy angels to conduct him to a place of refreshment, light and peace. Amen." [14]

It was suggested that this prayer be made daily by his friends for one hundred days.

Nor is the doctrine of hell believed in only by Roman Catholic Christians. It is found again and again in the responsive litanies read in many Protestant churches. The following prayer (and others of a similar vein), is found in the *Book of Common Prayer* used weekly in the Protestant Episcopal Churches of America and in the rituals of the Church of England:

"Remember not, O Lord, our offenses, nor the offenses of our forefathers, neither take thou vengeance on our sins. Spare us, good Lord, spare thy people whom thou hast redeemed with thy most precious blood, and be not angry with us forever."

Perhaps if this prayer were translated into the common language of everyday speech, it would not be so easy or seem so necessary to pray in these words. Just what is the suppliant asking of God?

6. Other Thoughts About Life After Death

Having criticized these old conceptions of heaven and hell, what more satisfying ideas have we to put in their place?

What would an ideal "everlasting life" be like?

Why have men so generally wished for "eternal life"?

Is death, in the world we know, a curse or a blessing?

This is a realm that has intrigued man's imagination from the beginning of thought. Many do their wondering in lonely silence, for the sense of the mystery of death is awesome, and because of our tradition it is sometimes fearsome as well. "When a man dies shall he live again?" is, however, a question which seems to have a universal appeal. When once we free ourselves from the feeling that it is a disagreeable or depressing subject to speak about, it may become a truly releasing experience to share honest questionings.

The subject grows in interest as one discovers the rich variety of ways in which people have imagined existence after death. Other legends explaining why men die have been told among other peoples than the Hebrews. Four such tales have been retold in *Beginnings of Life and Death*,[15] coming from the Greeks, the African Bushmen and the California Indians, as well as the tale of Adam and Eve. In this group, the story from the California Indians stands out as especially provocative since it does not explain the universality of the experience of death as a punishment inflicted by God, but as a natural and necessary compliment to birth. The Brothers Hus realize they must choose between the prospect of having their youth renewed from time to time and doing without children, or of growing old and dying but having the joy of children and the love that giving birth to them and caring for them brings. They choose to accept growing old and dying. Such an allegory, coming from a very primitive tribe of American Indians, has a fascinating appeal.

The different religions of the world have proposed different answers to this question that continues to elude human understanding. These are presented interestingly in the book *Questions That Matter Most: Asked by the World's Religions,* by Floyd H. Ross and Tynette W. Hills.[16]

The Buddhist parable, called *The Mustard Seed Medicine,* is the story of a young woman whose baby has just died. She begs Buddha to restore him to life. His reply and what the mother does are unforgettable. Lin Yutang calls this the most beautiful story that has come down to us from the ancient East. This is retold in *From Long Ago and Many Lands.*[17] The three books just mentioned are in the New Beacon Series in Religious Education, to which this present volume also belongs.

The following brief quotations are worth pondering.

Benjamin Franklin wrote his own epitaph: "The body of Benjamin Franklin, printer, like the cover of an old book—its contents torn out, and stripped of its lettering and gilding—lies here, food for worms. But the work shall not be lost, for it will, as he believed appear once more in a new and elegant edition, revised and corrected by the author."[18]

"Biological evolution can only continue, after a certain stage, by means of distinct individuals, limited both in space and in time. . . . We can say from an evolutive point of view the greatest invention of Nature is death"[19] (Lecomte du Nouy).

"For me life is a web and is immortal. . . . The web of humanity now on the loom of time, is but the end of the immeasurable sheet that recedes into the abysm of the past and the beginning of another to which we can see no end. . . . We survive, if we survive at all, only in the lives of our descendants. Every man and woman is born with the seeds of immortality within their bodies. . . .

"If the spirit of truth is the kernel of religion, then men of science are truly religious beings. They not only believe in the immortality of man, but they are convinced that this immortality is material."[20]

If death is like sound sleep unbroken even by a dream,
Then it is a wonderful gain. . . .
For in that case eternity is but a single night.

If on the other hand death is a journey to another world,
And if the traditional belief is true that all the dead are
    there,
What blessing would be greater than this?[21]

A class of boys and girls prepared their own original play on the life of the Pharaoh Akhenaton.[22] The leader of their dancing asked them if they thought they could express their own ideas about life after death in any kind of bodily movements. One boy impulsively offered to show his thought; after several measures of active skipping, he fell prostrate and lay completely motionless.

The leader then asked if any of the rest of the group could imagine some kind of living and moving *after* death. Another boy immediately started running and flapping his wings like an angel. This, of course, brought a laugh. "But do we really think that the idea of life after death is silly?" asked the leader. "Many people have thought very seriously about the matter." They then discussed briefly some of the movements they would make that would express their feelings about life now. After this preparation, the leader suggested a dance in three parts: first, life now; second, death; then, life after death. This suggestion had its appeal, so the leader invited them to try. The children spread themselves about the room. As she talked, the children moved, and the pianist followed with rhythms that harmonized with their movements. "The earth children skip their rhythm of life. They move happily and vigorously. . . . Sometimes they bump. . . . Sometimes they fall. . . . They are hurt . . . but they pick themselves up pluckily and go on in their skip of life till, as the years go on . . . old age slows their powers. . . . Death lays them to rest motionless. . . . Those who watch are sad . . . but a new life begins. . . . This time it is. . . ." Then she left the rest to the imagination of the dancers.

Three in the group created what was to the onlookers a deeply moving experience. Whitsie, a Chinese girl, walked serenely, slowly, in measured calm. Revelina, a Filipino, stood in one place and swayed like a lily in the wind, slowly spreading out her arms as if blooming in freedom. Arden, forgetting the silly flapping of wings, skimmed through space like a silver airplane.[23]

When one belongs to a group that is led by an encouraging and imaginative leader, unexpected and refreshing achievements often follow.

7. Chosen Peoples and Chosen Persons

Does God choose people today?

In the Story of Salvation, God works out his plan of salvation by choosing the people of Israel as his special beneficiaries, and within this nation God chooses special men to be leaders. The fairness of this general idea is likely to be questioned first when the stories of Jacob and of Joseph are read, because these two characters do not always seem to deserve their roles. The following conversation reveals the misgivings of a group of high school young people.

ELIZABETH: "Why would God choose a person like Jacob, who stole the birthright?"

ROBIN: "It's always the younger one who is favored."

HOLLY: "I don't think he was a very good God. But I don't think God is really like that."

ROBIN: "I think that Jacob should have loved all his sons the same. I would say Joseph was conceited."

HOLLY: "If I had a dream like that I wouldn't have told it."

(The teacher tried to explain the point of view of the author of the story—that God was using Joseph to accomplish his purpose, to save his "chosen people" from the punishment due them because of their sin.)

ELIZABETH: "Our constitution says that all men are created equal. Why does God pick out these certain people? But I guess we need rulers."

DIANA: "Yes, but our rulers aren't picked out by God but by the people. The mayor of our city doesn't think he was chosen by God."

ELIZABETH: "I think eventually we will all be equal."

In every period of history certain people stand out as playing especially significant roles. Let us try to understand why men used to say God chose this man or this people, and why today we are inclined to think that such persons *achieved greatness* rather than that they were sent into the world by God with a *greatness already assigned* to them.

Some will have an interest in learning a little of the history of the idea of a "chosen people." The Hebrews are not the only nation that has thought itself "chosen." Historians tell us that every great people of the ancient world at some time regarded itself as especially chosen by its deity for some great purpose that would raise it above other peoples.

The example most recently brought to our attention is that of the Japanese people. Their belief in their destiny was supported by their ancient Shinto theology. The Sun Goddess, Amaterasu, sent her son to the earth to be the first ruler of the Japanese islands.

In doing so she is reported to have said, "I think that this land will undoubtedly be suitable for the extension of the heavenly task, so that its glory should fill the universe. It is doubtless the center of the world." Until the end of World War II, every emperor who ruled Japan was regarded as descended directly from the Sun Goddess.

The people of Germany, Great Britain and America at one time or another have all thought of themselves as God's "chosen people." In fact when the Christian Church was established, it came to regard itself, rather than the Jewish people, as God's "chosen people," because, it was said, the Jews had rejected Jesus as their Messiah and no longer deserved God's special blessing.

To some people, this conception of God's having a "chosen people" whom he especially blesses and guides, seems immoral. Any person or people who think themselves thus especially chosen, they regard as arrogant. Do we see any way in which this idea may be revised so as to harmonize with our sense of justice?

8. The Crucifixion and Death of Jesus

Why did Jesus have to die? Did he know he was saving mankind?

It is important to distinguish between what this Christian tradition says was the reason for Jesus' death and what, historically speaking, can be regarded as the reason.

According to the tradition, Jesus died because God asked him to do so. God needed Jesus' help in order to do two things: first, to show God's condemnation of sin, thus proving that he is a God who cares for righteousness; and second, in order that God might be able to forgive sinful man rather than punish him eternally. This is the way St. Paul explained Jesus' death, and this explanation was accepted by the early Christian church. These ideas grew out

of the old custom of offering sacrifices to God as signs of repentance. The lamb or the ox suffered death, in place of the person
making the offering, in the hope that God would forgive the sin
by accepting the animal substitute and would not punish the man.
If then God planned that one great sacrifice should be made for
all mankind, surely a supremely valuable life had to be offered.
Only God's Son, a divine person, could be adequate for such great
forgiveness.

This reasoning seems crude to our generation because we have
come a long way from worshiping God by means of animal and
human sacrifices. But it was not a strange idea in the days when
Jesus lived and when the apostles worked out their beliefs about
Jesus.

Modern students are likely to question this whole conception
of Jesus' death. They ask the same kinds of questions regarding
Jesus' death that they ask regarding the death of any other martyr.
Why was Jesus opposed and hated by the religious leaders of his
time? Why did the Roman governor yield to the clamor of the
crowd for his crucifixion? Why did the Senate of Athens require
Socrates to drink the hemlock? Why was Gandhi assassinated?

When the gospel records are examined with a free and dis-
cerning mind, in order to discover the probable facts regarding
Jesus' teachings, it becomes clear, at least to many scholars, that
there was good reason for the Jewish leaders to wish to silence
Jesus. He was criticizing both the law and the temple rituals of
sacrifice. He also refused to play the role of Messiah that some of
his enthusiastic followers were urging him to assume in order to
lead their nation to victory against their Roman oppressors.

"By his specific teaching of non-resistance and love of enemies
(Mt. 5:39-44), he openly opposed the most deep-seated ambitions
of his people and denied them the bitter consolation, so often expressed in the Psalms, of wishing vengeance on their foes. . . . To
every patriotic Jew, Jesus' teaching could be taken as a betrayal

to Rome and, in this possibility alone, there was ample reason for the Jews to seek his death." So writes Dr. Leroy Waterman.[24]

Jesus lived during a period when this resentment of the Jews against their conquerors was burning violently. The Roman rulers were ever on the watch for any popular leader who was stirring up the people. Many trouble-makers, suspected of subversive activities, had already been crucified. Such an explanation of Jesus' death would seem justified.

Does it in any way belittle Jesus to consider his crucifixion a martyrdom due to human misunderstandings and fears? For many today, such an explanation adds to rather than subtracts from Jesus' stature. And even those who regard the supernatural meaning of the cross as vital to the Christian faith are moved by the poignant image of the brave and sympathetic man who paid the ultimate price for his beliefs.

When any one of us identifies himself with someone else who becomes his ideal, and then we see that ideal person go down in defeat, despised, rejected, his cause apparently lost, and at the same time we see that person triumphant, accepting the disaster bravely, believing there is a meaning in his unsuccessful struggle, such an experience does something to one's very soul. We can never be quite the same again. Our lives seem unimportant in themselves. We too become prepared to fail if need be. We too determine to give ourselves to the same cause and to continue the struggle.

Gandhi was a Hindu to the end of his life, but he found in Jesus' life and teachings and death this kind of salvation. It is said that his favorite Christian hymn was this one:

> When I survey the wondrous cross
> On which the prince of glory died,
> My richest gain I count but loss
> And pour contempt on all my pride.[25]

The cross of Christ, for thousands of others within and without the membership of the Christian Church, has symbolized this complete, unswerving commitment to what men have called "the will of God." Even though the Jesus of this Old Story of Salvation seems at some points to be out of tune with our modern thought, let us not superficially dismiss the Jesus of History. Let us remember also that the theologies that many have inherited and which they retain largely from a feeling of loyalty to their ancestors, are sometimes inferior to the values for which they actually live. The reality of the inspiration they have found in Jesus Christ is the secret to discover.

9.   *The Messiah or Christ and Jesus*

Did Jesus think of himself as the Jewish Messiah? Or as the Christ of the world?

What do these words mean?

Since the Greek language was the most popular language in the Middle East at the time the New Testament books were written, and since many Christians were Greeks, the Greek word for Messiah, namely "Christ," was substituted for the Hebrew word. This is why the term "Christ" has been added to Jesus' name rather than the term "Messiah." Putting the word into Greek made it possible also to put a broader meaning into the word "Messiah" than it had held for the Jews. For the Christian Church, Christ became the Savior of the world, rather than the Savior of the Jews first, and of the rest of mankind second.

The question that every serious student of the historical Jesus must ask is: Did Jesus think of himself as a Messiah or Christ in any meaning of those terms?

Those who have read the Old Story of Salvation will understand quite well the Jewish image of a Messiah which was common in Jesus' time. He was to be one sent from God who would save God's people from the hands of their enemies and would restore their independence. Since Israel's condition was so desperately weak, there could be no hope of such a salvation without God's supernatural intervention. Yet there were in Israel ardent nationalists who expected just such a sudden and powerful supernatural deliverance. This "son of the Most High," they believed, would "put down the mighty from their thrones" and exalt "those of low degree" (Luke 1:52). All rival powers would be put under his feet. His throne would be established in Jerusalem and his rule would have no end (Luke 1:33).

Jesus' disciples apparently were drawn to him because of their hope that he would prove to be the Messiah for whom the nation had been longing. There are a number of recorded episodes that reveal this attitude on their part. But Jesus' own thoughts about himself are not so clearly presented. Sometimes he is shown evading the question and sometimes he is made to contradict himself even within one sentence. This is why it is so difficult to decide just what Jesus thought about himself and what his disciples thought about him.

We can be thankful that, in spite of the biased points of view from which the gospels were written, glimpses have been preserved here and there of a Jesus whose original insights his disciples never grasped. In these passages, we find a Jesus who took the common slogan, the kingdom of God, that was continually stirring up the national passions of his people, and gave it an almost wholly different meaning. To Jesus, the kingdom of God was a personal spiritual experience of God's rule over one's individual life. It was a value a person must search for himself. It was like a lost treasure that needs to be found. Nor was it easy to find. There were some too blind to see it. Yet it was worth more than anything else in the world. Membership in the Jewish nation was no special asset. Some foreigners might find it more easily than some Jews.

This kingdom of God was not something God would send down from heaven by calling forth his hosts to conquer the kingdoms of the world. The kingdom of God was something to be taken hold of by each individual soul. It was within every man's grasp. Everyone had it in him to find it if he chose (Luke 17: 20-21).[26]

Nor would this kingdom come suddenly through violence. It would grow slowly and naturally as seeds grow. It could be found by those who had in them the spirit of children toward God, who accepted God wholeheartedly, lovingly and with truth. God's forgiveness comes even before it is asked for when such a spirit is in the individual.

But Jesus' disciples apparently sorely misunderstood him even to the end. His crucifixion came as a terrifying blow to their faith in him. They had thought he was the one who would redeem Israel and he had not done so. When the test came, God had apparently forsaken him.

Something, however, happened after Jesus' death to revive their hope. Just how it all came about, we shall probably never fully understand. It is apparent, however, that his disciples believed that Jesus was still alive even though he had been killed. Certain of them believed they had actually seen him and talked with him. They were assured that his death had after all been part of God's plan, that it was necessary for him to die as a ransom for the sins of the many. After a while when none among them reported having seen him, they concluded that Jesus had gone back to heaven. They insisted, however, that he had told them he would soon return to the earth again, even before any of them would themselves taste death, and then they would see the kingdom of God come with power (Mark 9:1).

But the years slipped by and Jesus did not return. All the while the determination of the Jews to free their nation from Roman bondage grew in intensity and finally exploded in a rebellion. The result was their total defeat and the utter destruction of the Temple and of the Holy City of Jerusalem in 70 A.D.

This terrifying disaster destroyed all hope of national independence, and it would have destroyed also all hope of a kingdom of God had it not been for the ardent faith and strong personality of one man, who is now known by the name of St. Paul. He had never seen Jesus, nor had he ever heard him preach. Paul was a Pharisee from Tarsus who came to Jerusalem to study, probably not long after Jesus' crucifixion. When he discovered a small group of visionaries who believed that Jesus was a crucified and risen Messiah, Paul became a furious Jesus-hater and led in the persecution of Christ's disciples.

But Paul soon had an unforgettable experience. He believed he heard Jesus speak directly to him and he was overcome. He fasted and struggled with his conscience and with his doubts, but finally he turned completely around and before long became the most effective of all the followers of Jesus. This was due to the fact that Paul worked out a philosophy regarding the significance of Jesus' death and resurrection that appealed to Gentiles, even though it never did win large numbers of the Jews. He saw the mission of Jesus Christ in world-wide terms, as a Messiah or Christ for the whole of mankind. Most of the Jews in Jerusalem were scoffing at the thought of their Messiah's having been crucified. Paul recognized that the very thought of a crucified Messiah was a stumbling block to them, yet to him it was a sign of God's deep wisdom (I Corinthians 1:18-25). God's plan was for all people—Jews and Gentiles alike. The Messiah had come for the salvation of the world. But his kingdom was *not of this world*. All material things would be destroyed *before* the kingdom of God would be established. The kingdom was not only a kingdom of heaven, but it was to be a kingdom *in* heaven.[27] To Paul, Christ was the first human being who had come back to life after having died. This was all-important. Christ had by this act proved his power to bring others back to life after death. He was able, therefore, to save mankind from the greatest of all enemies—death. This was the great curse which man had brought upon himself by his failure to obey God's law. Christ had ransomed man by taking the curse upon himself. God's gift of salvation was, therefore, the gift of eternal life (I Corinthians 15:12-24).

Thus a marked change took place in thought and belief regarding Jesus as the years went by. Jesus' own idea was that the kingdom of God was a personal spiritual value that everyone could find if he chose. It was something natural and possible in the here and now. The common thought of his lifetime disciples, however, was of a national and material kingdom that would grow to world-wide dimensions and would last forever. St. Paul's thought was different from either of these. He conceived of a spiritual kingdom, but one not of this world. It would be established not through men's efforts but through God's power, and would come only *after* all temporal things and all earthly governments had been destroyed. To Paul, the salvation Christ offered to those who would become one with him was the gift of eternal life.

The situation was doubtless not so simple as these brief statements would lead one to think. All New Testament students, however, will agree that the beliefs of St. Paul, in the main, became the most influential, not only during the first century or two, but that they have continued to represent the beliefs of the majority of Christian churches even down to the present time. It has often been said that St. Paul was the real founder of Christianity, and because of this it has been a religion *about Jesus,* the divine Savior, rather than the religion *of Jesus,* the man of history.

In order that we may understand why it is thought the disciples misunderstood Jesus and why there has been so much dissension among Christians and so much confusion in the thinking of church members throughout the centuries, it is desirable to know at least a little of how and when gospel records came to be written.

Jesus himself apparently never wrote anything. And contrary to a long held common belief, neither did any of his disciples. None of the gospels (at least in the form in which we now have them) was written by a companion or a contemporary of Jesus. The oldest gospel, Mark, was probably not written until thirty or forty years after Jesus' death. Papias, a Christian writer of the second century, spoke of its having been written by a man named Mark, "who had not heard the Lord, nor had he followed him."[28] It is thought that this Mark gathered most of his gospel from the stories he was able to get from Peter, who was then in prison in Rome. Peter's memories of what Jesus had said and done must have been influenced by the fact that for thirty or forty years he had been preaching the gospel of a risen Savior whose return he still expected in the near future.

When Matthew and Luke are compared with this earliest gospel, Mark, it becomes apparent that these authors copied it almost word for word. They omitted little, but they did add fresh material at certain points which suggests that they had found one or more other sources which are no longer in existence. They also made small changes here and there in the wording they found in Mark, sometimes changing the meaning only slightly, but sometimes adding a sentence or a phrase which made the meaning completely different.

Biblical scholars have also detected in all three of these gospels changes and additions that must have been made long after the gospels were first written. Some of these comments were apparently added by copyists even as late as the fourth century A.D.

And as for the gospel of John, it is commonly agreed that it was not written until the end of the first century or on into the second. The author says in his introduction that he made the record in order to prove that Jesus was the Christ, the Son of God. The order of events and the content of his book are both quite different from the other three gospels. Hence this gospel is accepted as a theological document rather than as biographical.

In view of such facts as these, one realizes that it is a difficult research task to discover the historical Jesus hidden beneath the contradictory and meager records. Yet the rank and file of us should not be too discouraged. If we secure such a book as *The Records of the Life of Jesus,* compiled by Dr. H. B. Sharman,[29] we can find out some very significant things for ourselves. In this book, the gospels of Matthew, Mark, and Luke are printed in parallel columns so that the records of any one episode can be compared easily. Every omission or addition or change from Mark can be seen. It becomes a fascinating detective adventure when one asks: Why did Luke omit this? Wasn't it in his copy of Mark? What reason could he have had for leaving it out? It is also possible to compare and contrast John's account, although that gospel appears by itself.

For example, it requires no special scholarship to notice, when the records arranged in this way are open before one, that Mark contains nothing regarding Jesus' birth. These miracle stories are absent from John also. Nor do we find in Matthew and Luke, after the telling of these stories, any reference to them in any later conversation by anyone. Why?

Again, the rite of baptism has been extremely important in the history of the church. Yet in Matthew, Mark and Luke there is not a single reference to Jesus' baptizing anyone. In fact the gospel of John says, "Jesus himself baptized not" (John 4:2). It is known that baptism was practiced when non-Jews were admitted into the Jewish national fold. It seems likely that Peter and the other preachers of Jesus as a Jewish Messiah used the rite when non-Jews were converted, but Paul wrote "God did not send me to baptize but to preach the good news" (I Corinthians 1:17). One wonders just why the Christian Church promoted the idea that Jesus instituted the rite of baptism?

Another very important command which the church has long assumed came directly from Jesus is what is commonly called "The Great Commission" (Matt. 28:19, 20; Mark 16:15, 16; Luke 24:46-49). Thousands of missionaries have gone into countries all over the world to preach the gospel because they have believed that this was Christ's last command and therefore his deepest desire.

But several facts have led many Biblical scholars to question whether Jesus himself ever commissioned his disciples to undertake such a world-wide preaching venture. For one thing, in the oldest gospel it comes in the last part of the last chapter of that gospel, in a section which is now generally recognized as a late addition to the original Mark. The translators of the Revised Standard Version of the Bible (1953) have put the ending of Mark, verses 9 to 18, in a footnote, indicating that they were not in the gospel as it was originally written. Apparently the author of this earliest gospel knew nothing of such a command. Indeed, this earliest gospel tells of no appearances of Jesus after his death. But Matthew and Luke both contain this "Great Commission," although the wording of the command differs in the two gospels. In Luke, Jesus commands that his disciples preach "repentance" and "the remission of sins," while in Matthew he commands them to "make disciples," baptizing them "in the name of the Father and of the Son and of the Holy Ghost." What a surprise these words bring! Here the doctrine of the Trinity is put into the mouth of Jesus himself. This is the only place in the entire New Testament where these ceremonial words are introduced. Historians say that it was not an accepted idea in Christian circles until A.D. 325. "When one has put all these findings together, it is natural to wonder: Did Jesus ever command his disciples to baptize? Did he ever command them to preach his gospel to the whole world? Can it be that the command came into the gospels through Paul? Could it be that he had thought he had heard the command from the one who appeared to him as he was going to Damascus? Was it Paul's idea, then, rather than that of Jesus?

Such questions and such a comparative examination of the gospel records is disturbing to one who is already convinced that the Christ of traditional Christianity is the Jesus of history. On the other hand, for those who have found the traditional picture of Christ confusing and unconvincing, such discoveries give glimpses of a more consistent and appealing personality. What kind of a person was Jesus really?

10.   Jesus and His Salvation

What then may *we* think of Jesus?
Is he our savior? And the savior of all men?
From what can he save us? And how can he do it?
Did Jesus think of himself as the Savior of the world?
Is this Jesus Christ the only hope of the world?
Can we save ourselves without a supernatural savior?
What have Unitarians meant by "salvation by character"?
Have men prayed to other saviors than Jesus Christ?
Can only one among these saviors be the true one?

In the light of what we already know and of what we still hope to learn, each one must think out for himself answers to these and other related questions. Some choose to use old words with new meanings. Others prefer new words for new meanings. Whichever may be our choice, all of us surely will wish to use words with clear meanings. The following comments and illustrations are intended merely as suggested starting points.

It was not only the early followers of Jesus who changed the religion *of* their master into a religion *about* their master. Buddha rebuked his disciples for even thinking that they could prove the truth of his teachings by doing miracles. Nor did he ever seek to have men worship him. Yet millions still pray to Buddha. It is fully as difficult to find the historical Buddha in the tangled web of miracle that has covered his life and teachings as it is to discover the historical Jesus. The quotation given below, taken from the Dhamapada, a book of Buddha's teachings, gives his clear call to the individual to use his own resources.

> By self alone is evil done:
> By self alone is one disgraced:
> By self is evil left undone:
> By self alone is one purified:
> Purity and impurity belong to self.
> No one can purify another.[30]

Is this a godless philosophy? Or a philosophy of deep faith? What resources does "the self" have? Is "the self" ever alone? What resources outside the self can be drawn upon? Can a community save an individual? Can an individual save a community? How? From what?

What may be gained through praying to a savior or to God for help? When may prayers become a way of avoiding personal responsibility?

A fifty-year-old rancher was talking intimately with a friend about many things, from politics to religion. He said he was really religious, although he seldom went to church. He said he prayed every day. And this was the substance of his prayer, as he gave it to his friend:

"Oh God! I don't know where you are. Some people know where you are, but I don't know. And I don't know what you look like. Everyone makes you look the way they want to, but I don't know what you look like. If I've done anything wrong today, I'll take the consequences. I just don't like to put anything on anyone else's shoulders. Amen."

Is the man arrogant? Or is he trying to accept himself and his personal resources fully?

And what shall we think of the world's other saviors? Is Jesus the only one who really has the power to save?

According to Peter, the disciple, "There is salvation in no one else, for there is no other name under heaven given among men by which we must be saved" (Acts 4:12). The author of the Gospel of John put this exclusive claim into the mouth of Jesus himself. "No one comes to the Father but by me" (John 14:6). It is hard to believe that a man like Jesus could have made such a claim. Most New Testament scholars today would not accept this as a genuine saying of Jesus.

But an exclusive claim for the Christian gospel has been commonly accepted as the Christian point of view. "Christ the hope of the World" was the theme of the gathering of the World Council of Churches in Evanston, Illinois, in 1954; by inference, Christ was regarded as the world's *only* hope.

As Dr. William Hocking points out, if one accepts the premises, the logic of the orthodox Christian foreign missionary enterprise is clear. (1) You presuppose that there has been a special revelation of God's great plan for mankind's salvation. (2) This plan could never have been known except through a particular act of God in which he presented his plan. (3) The alternative is eternal punishment or eternal death for all those who do not follow in this way. (4) Finally, God has given to human messengers the responsibility for warning mankind of its danger and of telling of the one way of escape. When once one accepts these premises, there is but one thing to do. "Go ye into all the world and preach the gospel."[31]

The liberal Christian group has been more tolerant than this. In fact there has been developing a new kind of Christian and missionary whose mind is open to new truth regardless of the religion from which it may come. This group finds some salvation in Buddha and Mohammed as well as some in Jesus Christ.

There are other stories of salvation told among other peoples in Asia, Africa and South America; men call upon the names of other saviors for salvation. The Hindus think of a number of saviors and of more appearing in times to come. It is reported that Krishna told his disciples that he would come again to the earth, not once but "in every age." His very last words are given as these:

> In every age I come back
> To deliver the holy,
> To destroy the sin of the sinner,
> To establish righteousness. [32]

Ever since their Lord Krishna lived, Hindus have been able to recognize a long succession of great personalities as saviors, from Rama and Buddha and Asoka and Jesus to Gandhi.

10.   The Unending Warfare Between God and the Devil

Is there a devil who has always been warring against God?
Is the devil as real as God?
Are there then two gods?
Must we be always fighting the devil? What does that mean?
This Story of Salvation is full of battles between "good people" and "bad people." Is that what life ought to be—fighting against "the bad" and fighting for "the good?"

Both Judaism and Christianity have been regarded as mono-theistic religions, yet in this Story of Salvation a secondary divinity is portrayed. The fundamental plot of the whole story is that of a long-drawn-out war between these two divinities. This conception of the devil was greatly influenced by the Zoroastrians of Persia. At sunrise one morning, Zoroaster conceived of Ahura Mazda as the God of Light and Goodness, and the coming of night suggested to him the God of Darkness as the God of Evil. Out of the experience of seeing light conquering darkness each morning, Zoroaster developed his belief in a similar battle in the spiritual world—the tension and rhythm of the victory of light over the dark—of good over evil.

The Christian Story of Salvation contains this same meaning and pattern for human existence. Man's one great and unending problem is: "Which god will I obey?" A well-known Christian hymn expresses the thought in this refrain:

"Who is on the Lord's side? Who will serve the King?"

In such a picture of the nature of a good life, the lines are clearly drawn between black and white alternatives, the good and the evil. Thus the world becomes a battleground. The "good" have the responsibility to fight the "evil," and the "evil" in turn must fight the "good." The commanders in these battles are God, the all-perfect and all-powerful one, and the devil, the all-evil one who is less powerful than God but who has more than human power. Complete victory is not promised until the end of the world. Even then, according to this Story of Salvation, the evil forces and the evil people will not be wholly destroyed, but will simply be made incapable of further resistance. "The hope of the world" turns into a hope for a divided humanity for all eternity—one part destined to live forever in bliss, the other part destined to a living death in isolated misery.

Is this the best we can hope for?

Are good and evil in real life distinguished so clearly in black and white colors?

Can evil be conquered as an enemy in battle?

Is evil destroyed by destroying the people who do evil?

What better ways did Jesus suggest? Or what better ways do modern psychiatrists suggest?

Has this long honored conception of life any relation to our difficulties in trying to avoid going to war?

11. What Then Do We Think of God?

If God represents our ideal of complete goodness—perfect love—is a second god needed to represent the opposite?
If God is pure goodness, how did evil come to be?
Is there some way of thinking of God so that divinity embraces all life?

It is all too rare an experience to find an adult who knows how to encourage a group who have begun to wonder seriously about God and who are eager to ponder and to exchange experiences and thoughts, yet who cannot profitably do so alone. The following report is an abridged and somewhat composite record of two such unusual experiences under the leadership of Dr. William A. Shimer.

On the wall in sight of all was hung a beautiful painting of Mt. Fujiyama, but it had been entirely covered by a piece of cloth. Since the young people had had more than one discussion on their own, and since they had invited Dr. Shimer to come, there was a feeling of keen expectancy in the air.

DR. S. "How many of you believe that there is a God?"
(Everyone responded in the affirmative.)
"Why do you believe there is a God?"
DANA. "There must be a force behind things, that people call God."
LEWIS. "So many people everywhere believe there is a God."
DR. S. "Let us start with ourselves, and see if we can get to God. Am I alive?"
SEVERAL. "I *guess* you are."
DR. S. "Why do you think so?"
DAVID. "You are talking."
DR. S. "The radio talks, too."
DANA. "But you are moving."

DR. S. "The Hudson River is moving, too.

Where do you really know what life is like?"

SEVERAL. "In nature. In yourself."

DR. S. "You really know about life because you yourself are alive. Others act as you do. And so you guess how they feel."

HARRY. "What does God look like?"

DR. S. "What does John look like? Could you describe what John looks like? Yes, you say, you can tell me the color of his eyes, and the shape of his nose and you can describe his face, and you can tell me how tall he is and what kind of clothes he wears, but would you be telling me what John is really like? There are many other things about John which we would not know anything about if we found out only what he looks like. In fact, the most interesting and important things about John we would not find out at all by knowing what he looks like.

"If we are not able to say very much about what John is like, how can we expect to be able to say what God is like? Yet perhaps we can tell as much about what God is like as we can tell about what John is like. For whenever we look at anything anywhere we are really seeing part of God, that is, we are seeing a part of God that can be seen, like John's body and clothes, and we have to guess about what we can not see."

TEACHER. "Primitive people say, 'God is everywhere, in trees and streams and fountains.' Is that different from what you are saying?"

DR. S. "The primitive people were close to the truth. A little knowledge fooled us. Scientists couldn't find God, so they once said 'There isn't any.' But primitive people *felt* there was more to their world than what they could see. They *felt* a god was here. Moses and Abraham and many others have felt the same way."

JANE. "But those primitive people thought there were many gods. How did God come to be just one?"

DR. S. "Because we have come to believe that this universe is united.

It is one and not many. (He dropped the piece of cardboard from which he had been reading occasionally and it fell to the floor.) What made this cardboard fall when I let go of it?"

EVERYBODY. "Gravity."

DR. S. "Is gravity only in this room? Is it only here on this earth to make us fall if we decide to go to the top of a big building and walk off? No. Gravity is everywhere. It is out in the great spaces where the stars are. Gravity is pulling all the time, and everywhere. It is always the same. It keeps the planets and the moon and the sun all moving around in an orderly way. So we believe that the universe all belongs together as one great unit. So if the universe is one, God is also one."

DANA: "Then where do you think God is, Dr. Shimer?"

DR. S.: "Where are you, Dana? Are you in your ear? In your finger? You are all over your body. So God is all over the universe. We have to guess about the part of God we can not see, just as we have to guess about the part of you we can't see. I think it is likely that God is in the life of the whole universe in the same way you are in your whole body."

HORACE: "If we can't see God, how do we know he is?"

DR. S.: "We were just saying that we could see what John's body is like, his face, his hands, his clothes, etc., but the best and most important part of John we never can see—his feelings and his thoughts. There is something about *life* that eyes simply can never see. So it is with God. We can see God's body, or his clothes, as it were, whenever we look around us, for God is the life in everything, everywhere. We ourselves are small parts of God. 'In him we live and move and have our being.' That is what St. Paul once wrote."

TOM: "Dr. Shimer, is the bad in us part of God?"

DR. S.: "If we are part of God, then we would have to say that the bad in us as well as the good is a part of God. Let us think of it this way. We have inherited from our ancestors a liking for sweets. Sweets give us one of the kinds of food we need. Now sweets are so easy for us to get these days that we sometimes eat too much, and that is bad. We do harm to our bodies. But the desire to eat sweets is not bad. It is something natural in us that can be used in a good way or in a poor way. When we do not control our appetites we do what is bad, but that does not mean that God is bad, for the desire for sweets that is given us really helps us to find what we need to keep well."

Tom: "Why do we pray? How do our prayers get to God?"

Dana: "I guess it's like talking to yourself."

Dr. S.: "That would do partly."

Then Dr. Shimer stepped in front of the covered painting.

Dr. S.: "You are curious to know what sort of a picture is behind this cloth, aren't you? I will lift this small corner. Seeing this small part, what do you imagine the whole painting is about?"

The boys and girls began guessing. Dr. Shimer slowly lifted the cover farther. The boys and girls made more guesses. Gasps of surprise came when he had lifted the covering completely.

Dr. S.: "Now let us suppose that instead of this painting of Fuji-yama, we have before us a great big painting of the whole universe. Let us suppose the painting is alive. All the people of the world, all the animals—everything, everywhere—are in this picture. We are in it, too, down in one small corner. We keep making new pictures all the time as we move about and do things. But each one of us can see only a very small part of the great picture.

"How would you feel being in such a great painting? What would you be wondering about? or wishing for?"

Children: "We'd want to know more about the rest of the paint-ing."

"We'd wonder how we got into the painting."

"We would want to know what we were a part of."

DR. S.: "Yes, we'd want to know more about the kind of painting that was being made, so that we would know how to paint our part well rather than have the whole painting spoiled by some messy spots we made. If then we think of God as being perhaps a little like the great Artist who began the great painting, we would want to tell God in some way that we really want to understand more about the great painting. And this would be one way of praying.

"This is the kind of praying a scientist does whenever he looks into a microscope to find out something. Whenever an astronomer looks through a telescope in order to learn more about the stars, he is really praying.

"I do not mean, of course, that the scientist always says a prayer in words when he looks into a microscope or through a telescope. I mean that his earnest desire to know more is itself a prayer.

"We do not expect God to hand out answers to our questions, nor do we expect him to whisper an answer to us. We know we must study, and read, and look, and think, and experiment in order to know more. We want to understand more of what everything is about so that we can know what we should be about. We want to plan our living so as to help rather than to spoil this very wonderful living, growing life of which we are small parts. Although we may never know everything, we are always hoping to know more. This kind of praying, I think, we will never want to give up as long as we live."

After the session was over, these were some of the comments:

DEAN: "O boy, wasn't that good? It cleared up a lot of things for me."

JIMMIE: "But wasn't it tantalizing?"

CHARLES: "That man certainly knows how to explain things."[33]

A belief in God such as was expressed by the leader of this

discussion may seem to some to be too ethically neutral and vague to provide the needed authority for righteous living, or to awaken the love that the God of the Story of Salvation has brought to millions of believers. On the other hand, the thought of such an inclusive, indwelling, and natural yet overarching divinity may bring to others an exhilarating feeling of being trusted by the all-embracing life-giver, of being given the dignity of having a creative, original part to play in the magnificent drama of life. Such a religious philosophy, so vividly opened up to these young people, enables one to believe that the problems of evil can be solved in the here and now. Such a faith lures one on in the search to find the solutions. Pain and sorrow and evil are recognized as necessary parts of the whole. Being accepted, they can be transformed. The uncompromising *either/or* between "the good" and "the evil" is supplanted by a realistic effort to understand and sympathize with people's needs and desires. The fight between "good" and "evil" becomes transformed into an intelligent and reasonable balancing of values. God, the lawgiver, the one whose will man must obey or die, becomes a creating, growing God with whom man may participate in lesser acts of creativity. Such a revised thought of God seems to harmonize well with modern man's growing recognition of the need to be less rigid and less condemning in his attitude toward "wrong." It spurs him to learn the artistry of sympathetic understanding and negotiation between differing interests and needs.

Were the secret thoughts of the great theologians fully revealed, we would probably discover that none of them felt he had been able to formulate a fully satisfying belief regarding God. It would seem to be in the very nature of humanity that this is impossible. The truly religious person is seldom dogmatic, and even those who may at times seem to be so, will at other times transcend their dogmatism both in the tenderness of their sympathies and in their more intimate expressions of thought.

St. Paul and St. Augustine are both appealing examples of this kind of inconsistency. When St. Paul stood with some Greeks before an altar in Athens, he spoke of God as the one "in whom we live and move and have our being," and in that belief he found common ground with them (Acts 17:28). St. Augustine at one time wrote, "Nothing is to be accepted save on the authority of Scripture, since greater is that authority than all the powers of the human mind."[34] Yet at another time he wrote wistfully that God is like a great circle, whose center is everywhere and whose circumference is nowhere[35]—a thought as all-inclusive and vague and mystical as the one suggested in the discussion reported.

Shall we then stop trying to think or talk about God? Some would say "Yes," for when a person has once defined God to his satisfaction, his awareness of the reality—God—has been lost. The Zen Buddhists say, "The Tao that can be expressed is not the eternal Tao."

But is the real choice between thinking about God and feeling the reality—God? Should not the heart and mind be wedded in harmony? Is it possible to be without some thought of this Reality —God— "in whom we live and move and have our being," without having our emotions involved? The real choice we must make is between poor thinking and good thinking, between having feeling experiences with what is in truth reality and having feeling experiences with what we mistake for reality or what we may wish were reality. If we stop thinking, we will simply go on living with the last thought we had. Unfortunately this is just what many do. They live with outworn religious ideas, while at the same time they speed ambitiously to grasp the latest ideas in every other realm of life.

But thinking about God requires questioning, doubting what has been thought, and facing the threats of failure and non-conformity. Christianity has been so certain of its thought patterns for so long that it has discouraged original inquiry. To have the

right belief has been set forth as the price that must be paid for
salvation. The best in us cries out for freedom to change, even
though it means being always unsatisfied. "Our life is an appren-
ticeship to the truth that around every circle another can be drawn;
that there is no end in nature but every end is a beginning; and
that there is always another dawn risen on mid-noon, and under
every deep a lower deep opens." [36]

12.   A Summary

What then are the great ideas which this Old Story of Salvation expresses?

Which of these great ideas have proved to be harmful?

Which of these ideas seem to be true to our experience, and
beneficial to live with?

And are there greater ideas that we glimpse rising above the
horizons of our thinking?

The Old Story of Salvation
in the Arts

The Story of Salvation in Literature

References to this or that incident or idea in this Old Story of Salvation are to be found in multitudes of books—ancient and modern. In fact, no one can read English literature intelligently unless he is familiar with this story. These references appear in novels, books of history, devotional books, essays, and even in books of psychology and sociology.

A few outstanding classics portray its most dramatic scenes. The most popular book of this type is *The Pilgrim's Progress* by John Bunyan, written in jail about 1670.[37] For at least two hundred years it was a bestseller, having been translated into almost as many languages as the Bible itself. *The Pilgrim's Progress* is an allegory in the form of a dream, dramatizing the emotional struggle of a believer, burdened with sin and fear, seeking salvation. It portrays Christian's flight from the City of Destruction and his long and arduous pilgrimage to the Celestial City.

There was a time when every English school boy or girl was familiar with the important characters in this allegory: Mr. Worldly Wise Man, Mistrust and Pliable, Faithful and Little Faith, Ignorance, Mercy, Stand Fast, Madam Bubble, Giant Despair, Mr. Money Love, Great Heart and Valiant for Truth. And he could himself dream of the places to which Christian came—the Slough of Despond, the House Beautiful, the River of Death, the Delectable Mountains, Doubting Castle and the Celestial City.

Modern reprints of this old classic are available in attractive form with the same fascinating line drawings that were in the original editions.[37] No book will so quickly put one into the atmosphere of the Old Story of Salvation as will *The Pilgrim's Progress*.

Two other great English classics whose dramatic scenes were built on this Old Story of Salvation are John Milton's *Paradise Lost* and *Paradise Regained*. These, however, require considerable intellectual maturity and scholarship to read.

The Story of Salvation in Music and Song

Some of the world's greatest oratorios portray in music scenes from this Story of Salvation, such as Handel's *Elijah* and *Messiah*, Bach's *Matthew's Passion*, and *The Magnificat;* many of the great organ pieces played during the celebration of the Mass or at Protestant Communion services; the rich repertoire of Christian choir music and chorals; and the Christmas and Easter carols sung to celebrate the two most significant scenes in the Story of Salvation. Had not Christians for generations believed and loved this Story of Salvation, such music would never have been created. "Silent Night! Holy Night!" "Star of wonder! Star of Light!" "Hark the herald angels sing!" "Christ the Lord is risen today. Hallelujah!" The hymns sung in Christian churches the world over are full of pictures and ideas taken from the Story of Salvation.

> Just as I am without one plea,
> But that thy blood was shed for me.
>
> Throw out the life line!
> Some one is sinking today.

Mine eyes have seen the glory of the coming
    of the Lord.

Onward Christian soldiers! Marching as to war.

His blood stained banner streams afar.
Who follows in his train?

The Negro spirituals, so moving and beautiful in their simplicity,
were the heartfelt outpourings of believers in this gospel story.
    Sinner, do you love my Jesus?

We are climbing Jacob's ladder.

Go down Moses! Let my people go!

Get on board the gospel train.

How often we sing the words of such songs as these without
thinking what we are saying!

It would be a worthwhile experiment to go through the
hymnal or song book used in your own church or synagogue and
see how often ideas from this Story of Salvation appear.

The Story of Salvation in Painting and Sculpture

Ever since the time when Europe built its first cathedrals
and monasteries, most of the best art of the West has been moti-
vated by this Story of Salvation. The personalities and the scenes
of the story, and symbols of its thoughts, have been portrayed in
painting, sculpture and in stained-glass windows. Beautiful printed
copies of many of these great masterpieces can be seen or pur-

chased. Samples of these are on display in the great museums of the West and are also available in beautifully illustrated books, several of which are listed in the appendix.[38]

The Story of Salvation in Drama and Dance

Since the vast majority of Christian people in the West remained illiterate and without books during the first seventeen hundred years and more of the church's history, it became necessary to present the gospel through as many of the visual arts as possible. As early as the fifth and sixth centuries, wise bishops and priests ventured to make the services of worship more interesting to the average person by having "living pictures" presented in the sanctuary itself to illustrate one by one the particular sentences in the Latin litanies.

Later, from the eleventh through the sixteenth centuries, these simple tableaux flowered into extended religious dramas called "mystery plays." In these, all the crucial scenes in the drama of salvation were enacted, sometimes in the churches themselves, but even more often in the out-of-doors on the streets and in public squares. Sometimes movable stages were wheeled from one cross-roads to another so that everybody would be sure to see at least one of the scenes in the drama. These "mystery plays" are sometimes called "miracle plays" also, but this latter term was first used to describe those plays which presented stories of the miracles of the saints rather than stories from the Biblical drama.

A second type of religious drama, called "morality plays," was also developed during this period. These plays were allegorical. The characters represented the virtues and vices of men. The theme running through all these "morality plays" was basically the theme that pervades the Story of Salvation—namely, the conflict between God and the Devil or, in abstract terms, the conflict between good and evil.

The yearly Christian festivals of Christmas and Easter have afforded the church its greatest opportunities to present dramatically the great scenes in the Story of Salvation. For centuries Christmas crèches, with their clay figures of the holy family, the angels and shepherds and wise men, have been set up in thousands of homes and churches. Processions of worshipers still go annually in imagination to the manger in Bethlehem, with torches and candles and gifts for the "king." Over and over at Easter time, the scenes of Good Friday and of the day of resurrection are re-enacted. The sacred body of Christ may lie symbolically buried in a coffin throughout the hours of Saturday, while church bells toll in mourning. Then, just before midnight or before the dawn on the first day of the week, this coffin may be carried out, perhaps to the open village square, behind a procession of mourning worshipers. Then at the stroke of the hour, a trumpet will be blown and a priest will call the glad tidings, "Christ is risen!" The church bells will break into quick, strong peals, and the people will greet each other with the happy words, "Christ is risen!" The crowds will burst into song, and sometimes fire crackers will be exploded.[39]

The Story of Salvation in Modern Art Forms

It is not in the old and traditional art forms only that these beliefs and feelings are now being expressed. The modern artist, dramatist and dancer are giving new forms of expression to these old themes. In a growing number of these modern paintings and sculptured figures, the symbolism of this old drama is being given fresh expression. The personalities of the story are being portrayed with a new sensitiveness to the intangible essence of the spirit, and sometimes with a vivid naturalism. The agony of the crucifixion is so relentlessly portrayed that to look upon it is like having a sword thrust into one's own bosom. And some modern painters are attempting to portray new symbolic imaginings even of heaven.

Amateur groups in our church schools, studying this Story of Salvation, have sometimes painted their own murals on long stretches of manila paper, depicting scenes from these seven ages of time. Others have shown by means of symbolic lines and colors the heights and the depths of feeling that the story expresses—the rhythmic movement from encouragement and uplift to rejection and despair—as these return over and over at the beginning and the end of each age.

And the art of the dance is now being revived as a legitimate form of religious expression. As long as the old ideas still live in our culture, these will continue to find expression in new forms of art, although with some revisions in the ideas as well as in the art forms.

At the assembly in Evanston, Illinois, of the World Council of Churches, in the summer of 1954, one hundred twenty-five thousand ministers and Christian laymen from all over the world gathered in the open stadium of Soldier Field in Chicago. As the climax of this stirring meeting, a skilled group of dancers presented on the stage the six greatest scenes of crisis from this Old Story of Salvation: the creation of the world, the fall of Adam and Eve, the birth of the Christ, his death, his resurrection, and finally his second coming and the Day of Judgment.

Some, in reporting the meeting, said that the most memorable moment of exaltation came when the entire gathering of one hundred twenty-five thousand people rose and sang Charles Wesley's old hymn:

> Jesus shall reign where'er the sun
> Does his successive journeys run.
> His kingdom stretch from shore to shore
> Till moons shall wax and wane no more.

Some fortunate groups of young people have had the inspiration and guidance of religiously-minded teachers of the modern dance, who understand how to encourage untrained persons to express their feelings in bodily movement. Some groups in our churches have worked out for themselves dance forms to express not only the feelings that permeate this Story of Salvation, but also the emotional movements of the contrasting Story of Evolution and the long-time hope of mankind for one world community of friendly peoples.

Two classes of boys and girls who had studied both this Old Story of Salvation and the scientists' Story of Evolution prepared as a climax to their period of cooperative work two original dances. One class expressed in bodily movement, to the accompaniment of improvised piano music, the emotional levels in the Old Story of Salvation. They began with a dance to express the joy of a "Golden Age" and God's pleasure in seeing that his creation was good. Then with Adam and Eve's disobedience, the emotional tone suddenly dropped to one of shame and bitterness. After struggling with work and pain and sickness and jealousy, mankind began slowly to regain hope, but then came the world-wide flood, and man reached the depths of tragedy. Again, the dancers showed the slow rise of hope with the choosing of Abraham and his descendants as the vehicles of God's divine grace. Soon, however, the dancers once more bent low to express the years of slavery in Egypt, until hope came again with the appearance of Moses. So with the coming of each new age, hope rose, and yet before the age was ended tragedy and despair returned. The progress of the drama was presented with these exultant and depressed movements alternating, until the high climax came with the resurrection of Christ. Then the final age was depicted as ending in the stern Day of Judgment, with part of the group being lifted up into a life of happiness and the remainder sinking in agony into a place of hopelessness and torture forever and ever.

The second group presented in contrast the emotional levels represented in the scientists' Story of Evolution, beginning with the low forms of life and crude self-centered activities—bumping and hitting. Slowly new and more complex forms rose; some stagnated and remained unchanged, and some disappeared, but in general the dance of evolution represented a slow rising, with some backward movements as well as forward ones, and some fallings as well as risings. The whole dance ended on a note of hope and a feeling of togetherness, with the impression that there would be no end. Even though the young people felt awkward in trying to present such feelings in dance form, they enjoyed the experiment. An artistically skilled production was not the goal. Indeed, the very fact that it was amateurish tended to accent the honesty of the experience.

For the assembly in which these dances were presented, a committee from the two classes had prepared a responsive reading to be used after the dances. The two groups in the assembly read the alternating statements, "It was said by them of old" and "But we say today." In the brief sentences following a repetition of these two introductory phrases, the young people summed up a half dozen of the main ideas in the Old Story of Salvation. Each of these was followed by a contrasting statement of their own thinking in the present. It was an impressive assembly for those who were guests and a richly educative and emotionally satisfying experience for the boys and girls who prepared it.

What our ancestors achieved in the arts to express their religious beliefs was indeed extraordinarily beautiful. They fittingly expressed the noblest sentiments in this Old Story of Salvation. But what the present and future generations may do is more than beautiful. It is prophetic.

What Then Shall We Do with This Old Story of Salvation?

This is indeed a serious problem for individuals and for the Christian Church to face. Probably the number of persons who believe that the whole story from beginning to end is literally true is comparatively small. Even St. Augustine, who lived in the fifth century, wrote, "To believe that God formed man from the dust with bodily hands is very childish. . . . God neither formed man with bodily hands nor did he breathe upon him with throat and lips."[40] But if all of it is not literally true, what is there in this Story of Salvation that is true?

The very fact that so many differing positions are being taken regarding this Christian tradition is evidence that many people are struggling with the problem: on the one hand, to preserve the cherished values which still live in the "faith of our fathers," and, on the other hand, to adjust the faith they themselves live by to advancing knowledge. Instead of separating ourselves into debating societies, each intent on defending its own point of view, let us take our differences as evidence of our need to keep together in order that we may understand each other and garner the best out of our variations.

Although it is quite unfair to catalogue a person according to the way he once advocated dealing with this Story of Salvation, yet it seems desirable to separate some of the outstanding ways by noting their differences, knowing full well that few individuals will fit neatly into any one of these categories. In this spirit, therefore,

177

let us examine seven of the ways in which this Story of Salvation is regarded today.

1. The Way of Complete Rejection

The way of complete rejection of this Christian tradition is the way which most of us would like to avoid. It seems unappreciative and shallow, yet it is unfortunately the way to which many men and women have been emotionally driven because of the violence of their protest against dogmatic evangelism, or against what seemed to them meaningless rituals. Feeling imprisoned by imposed patterns of belief or deadened by the repetition of "vain words," they have had to escape into a non-religious society. Discarding the framework of the Christian faith, they have felt constrained to discard *all* religious faith. Having been repulsed by the image of God which they saw dominating this Christian tradition, they have rejected the possibility of any belief in God. Having been repelled by the stories from the Bible which they heard in childhood, they have lost all desire to study the book as adults. Some of these protesters have grown to understand their emotions, and they have been able to move forward toward the finding of a faith that seems to them more worthy of advancing insights. Those who are still compelled merely by their negative emotions are like workmen who have destroyed a building, but who have never cleared away the debris and started a new structure.

2. The Way of Evangelistic Affirmation

The way of affirmation characterizes large groups within both Catholic and Protestant churches. Beliefs about God, Christ, the chosen people of God, salvation, heaven, and hell, as presented in this Story of Salvation, are assumed, not discussed. The gospel of salvation "through Jesus Christ our Lord, the hope of the world," is proclaimed.

Such assurance adds to the fervor of the evangelist and strengthens his appeal. When this Story of Salvation is presented in the name of a time-honored institution such as the Christian church, men are humbled, convicted of sin, and stirred to repentance. The gospel actually preached may vary in some details—certain parts may be emphasized by one preacher and other parts by others, yet the message as a whole is still the old gospel. The growth of Christianity has been due in large measure to the fact that Christians have believed that they have a true "story to tell to the nations," and that Christ's last command to his disciples was to preach this salvation to all creation.

This point of view is clearly shown in a quotation from the message prepared by a highly qualified group of leaders in the Protestant world for the consideration of the representatives of the World Council of Churches meeting in August, 1954, in Evanston, Illinois:

"The Cross is that place at the centre of the world's history where the Lord of history has finally exposed the sin of the world, and taken that sin upon himself, the place where all men and all nations, without exception, stand revealed as enemies of God, lovers not of truth but of the lie, children not of light but of darkness, and yet, where all men stand revealed as beloved of God, precious in God's sight, children for whom the Son of God was content to die. It is the crucified Lord who is the hope of the world."[41]

This is a carefully worded summary of the Story of Salvation, set forth with assurance; yet even this was questioned and slightly revised by the members of this great gathering.[42]

3. The Way of the "Social Gospel" and of Idealism

The great prophets of Israel, and Jesus himself, insisted that "to do justice and to love mercy" is more than "all burnt offerings and sacrifices." The vigorous preachers of this "social gospel," especially honored during the first three decades of our century, encouraged the churches to participate in significant social reforms. The teachings of Jesus were seriously examined and held up for emulation. By shifting the center of interest from doctrine to social action, these socially minded prophets led the churches to feel that it was more important to struggle to make society more Christian than it was to struggle to reform the traditional theologies.

Nevertheless, this ethical emphasis led naturally to some revisions in the old Augustinian model of the Story of Salvation. It turned people's attention away from the Old Testament toward Christ. The Sunday school lesson materials prepared by the denominations became Christ-centered. The Old Testament had value only as an introduction to the New. Christ was no longer the divine Son sacrificed to satisfy God's stern sense of justice and the belief that all sin must be punished in order to prove that God himself is good. Instead, Christ became the revelation of the forgiving and loving spirit that, it was said, had been in God all the time, although men had failed to recognize it. Christ was not a sacrifice offered to appease God's wrath. Christ became the very revelation of God himself. God was seen by seeing Christ. Christ showed what God was like when a man, and what God wants all men to be like. The gospel story thus became a gospel of idealism. God became man's highest ideal of love, and Jesus Christ made that ideal concrete in his life and death.

Jesus' death then was the result, not of God's demanding it, but of the conflict between Jesus' ideals and the passions of evil men. Jesus Christ suffered as all good men suffer for the sins of others in a sinful world. Christ suffered as fathers and mothers suffer for the sins of their children, and as children suffer for the sins of their parents. Sacrifice is the natural price paid by love in a sinful world. Christ's crucifixion became the example or symbol of perfect and complete love—the love of God.

Most Christians were probably quite unaware of how this ethical emphasis had changed the old version of the Story of Salvation. Many had never had the old version presented to them so that they could see the contrasts. The evasion of theological issues in the church's educational work, however, opened this group of liberal socially minded pioneers to the criticism of being superficial, of seeing life in too optimistic a light, of thinking primarily of ideals and of disregarding present realities. They were accused of talking too easily of God's love and of omitting sin and judgment, of forgetting the tragic dilemma that man's sinful nature presents to every soul, of not being aware of the ugly emotional depths in which idealism is drowned. So the pendulum of concern swung back to theology in an effort to harmonize Christian faith with the fresh understandings of the teachings of Jesus and the prophets.

This way of accenting the "social gospel," with its interpretation of the loving Christ as the revelation of God, added a new warmth to Christian ardor and a fresh vitality to the church.

4. The Way of Seeking Truths in Mythology and Legend, as Well as in History

As the sciences of history, of archaeology, of Biblical criticism, and the natural sciences advanced, the Christian church was compelled to readjust its understanding of the ancient Biblical records. The stories of creation, of the flood, of the Tower of Babel, and many of the miracle tales were clearly either myths or legends, and many inaccuracies and inconsistencies were pointed out when duplicate versions of the same episode were compared. The difficult question that these advances in knowledge raised was this: If one accepts the validity of these findings, how much of the Old Story of Salvation is left that can still be proclaimed as true?

The way which many scholarly men are following today is to find in the myths and legends deeper truths than mere historical records can represent. To them, myths are not simply fanciful tales; they put into dramatic form or into symbols deeper insights into the nature of God and man than history alone can do. The myth of Adam's fall, they say, presents in an unforgettable way certain basic truths regarding human nature and God. It does not matter whether or not there ever was an Adam or Eve or how long ago they were created or how. They are but symbols of all mankind, and it is "the truths" behind the myth regarding God and man which are important.

Looking at the climax of the salvation drama in Jesus Christ from this general point of view, it is accepted that the historical Jesus must have been quite a different person from the deified Savior of this Christian tradition. These theologians, however, would say that the Christ of the Church represents a deeper insight into the nature of the Jesus who lived than we can ever hope to find through any further study of history.

Taking the Bible as a whole, this group of theologians say that what the Bible tells about man's history may not be accurately presented, and its science may be antiquated; but what the Bible reveals about God and his way with men can be called "truth." Behind these varying and even contradictory words of men, these interpreters still believe they find "the word of God."

This so-called "modern liberalism" still accepts the really basic ideas in the Old Story of Salvation (with varied modern re-interpretations of their meanings) without accepting all the concrete details as history. They spurn the thought of any literal concept of inspiration, yet they can still speak of the Bible as God's "self revelation" because it gives "the deepest interpretation of our own life situation and our world crisis in the twentieth century." From this point of view, the Bible again becomes a unity. The God of Genesis is the God of Jesus. The Bible gives a "forward-moving drama of God's action in the history of his people, Israel . . ." toward that climax which is the "good news" of the New Testament. Thus the Bible does not present primarily man's search for God, but God's search for man. This point of view is presented in *Rediscovering the Bible,* by Dr. Bernhard W. Anderson, Dean of Drew Theological Seminary.[43]

To those who take another point of view regarding this Story of Salvation, this way of mythologizing seems confusing. It is difficult to explain to children and even to most adults. Some Biblical scholars are disturbed also because the prevalence of this point of view at the present time seems to be weakening interest in the laborious search for the actual history behind the Biblical writings. Furthermore, it tends to induce both Old and New Testament scholars to withhold clear and full reports of their studies from popular knowledge, lest Christian foundations be shaken. If the "lessons" or "truths" to be learned from history are accepted prior to an investigation of the facts, the desire to know the facts is weakened. When the accent is put on the "truths" in the symbols rather than on the true history, one is left without a way by which to test the truth of the "truths." How can the truth of any myth or legend be tested or rightly understood, without appealing to actual human experience—which the true historian aims to present?

5. The Way of Allegory

The way of mythologizing leads on for some into the way of allegory. The entire Story of Salvation, although intertwined with history when it was first conceived, is now regarded by some as an allegory presenting symbolically the journey of the individual soul from eternity to eternity. This understanding of the gospel story is not new. It was unforgettably portrayed in Bunyan's *The Pilgrim's Progress*. Christian flees from the City of Destruction, burdened by a heavy load of sin on his back. After many trials he reaches the place where the cross stands beside an open tomb. His burden falls from his back and rolls into the tomb. Christian then journeys on with a light heart. In the end he crosses the Jordan and is welcomed into the Celestial City of God.

With this allegorical interpretation, the majestic drama that embraces the whole human race pictured in a cosmic setting, is reduced to the personal drama of each individual life. All men become one man. The living Christ becomes the personal Savior, and the hour of death becomes the Day of Judgment.

Such an interpretation makes it possible to disregard all the actual historical events in the framework of the salvation drama, and to reinterpret its meanings in the light of modern insights gained through the psychological approach to the understanding of human need. The old terms—sin, repentance, salvation—can be reinterpreted in terms of compulsive hostilities, feelings of guilt and inferiority, and the release of the spirit through self-understanding and self-acceptance, on the assumption that divine or supernatural help is both needed and available.

The possibilities in this way of interpreting the Old Story of Salvation are richly suggested in *Myth and Ritual in Christianity* by Alan W. Watts, an author well versed in the history of Christianity and other religions, and one who understands the significance of depth psychology.[44]

6. *The Realistic Way of Learning About Man's Historical Experiences*

A realistic way of dealing with this Old Story of Salvation is to submit it to an objective examination, and to separate the facts of history from the mythical and theological interpretations of those facts as given in the Bible, and then to gather together what there is in the story that is historically true, and to correct what is not true.

This way involves searching the Biblical records with utter candor, on the assumption that these books were produced by human beings and are about human beings basically like ourselves. It means correcting and supplementing our understandings by making use of knowledge gained from other sources. It means having confidence in what true history can contribute toward present living.

This realistic approach involves more than a superficial gathering of facts. It calls for a sensitive searching to understand men's emotional experiences, an appreciation of both their tragic needs and their glowing dreams. It means identifying oneself emotionally with the personages of history. Those who advocate this realistic way would not belittle the emotional elements in the drama or fail to find value in symbols. They intend merely to try to discriminate between an objective record of historical experience and any one interpretation of that experience.

These realists recognize also that these Biblical records came out of one small section of humanity and grew and developed in one small part of the world. For them the experiences of one people alone are not enough to know. They would, therefore, compare this Jewish-Christian Story of Salvation with similar stories coming from the histories of other peoples, from the Hindus, the Buddhists, the Moslems, the Iroquois Indians and the Indians of South America, and others.

Such a realistic way of dealing with this Old Story of Salvation within the framework of a world-wide history has led to the raising of certain very vital questions regarding "the truths" that are so commonly assumed as forming the heart of the story. These questions have already been raised in the first section of Part II. When these have been considered carefully, the question naturally emerges: How many of these basic ideas can be revised or discarded without destroying the essence of the story as a whole?

This realistic way of dealing with the Story of Salvation is fraught with real danger to the survival of Christianity, or at least so it would seem to many. Yet if Christians try too hard to save Christianity, may they not lose that which they try to save? There may be a corollary here to the words of Jesus. That religion which seeks to save itself may lose the very life it has, but that religion which is ready to lose itself may save the life-giving element within it.

7. The Way of Searching for New Insights

This seventh way of searching for new and truer insights—seeking to find a truer story of man's destiny and hope—is a way that calls for a courageous, creative adventure, involving much sharing of knowledge and experience. Those who no longer find the symbols and the myths and "the lessons" embodied in this Old Story of Salvation expressive of truth as they see it or inspiring to live by, are naturally left wishing for something else equally powerful in its emotional appeal to take its place. They feel a need for new words and new art forms, new symbols and new allegories, and a new history and new prophesies to express their deepest and most strengthening thoughts. They believe that sound understandings can be built only on sound thinking and sound knowledge regarding both the depths of personal experience and the breadths of universal experience.

Our generation needs to investigate and to live with the scientists' imaginative pictures of the universe and of mankind's ages of evolution. We need to listen to their prophesies of man's possible destinies and prepare to face them. The rank and file of us need to familiarize ourselves with the accounts of the history of man that the biologists and sociologists and anthropologists and historians are constructing. We need to be on the alert for their interpretations of the meanings they find in this great human drama, and the signs of promise they discern.[45] A greater story of salvation is in the making. In our age and time, the plot is moving at an accelerated pace. We seem to be facing terrifying alternatives. Wherein lies our hope?

These then are seven of the characteristic ways men have been taking in dealing with this ancient Story of Salvation. There are no doubt other ways that have escaped our awareness, and there are no doubt quite a few variations of point of view within these seven categories. The fact that so many different ways are being tried by which to preserve its values shows that Christians of our time are taking more seriously their need to think on the large problems involved in the development of a reasonable personal religious philosophy of life. Our very differences are signs of vitality, provided we are unafraid to reveal them to one another. It is encouraging to recognize that our generation is changing in deep ways as well as in those ways that are easily observed by ear and eye.

The questions to be thought through are ones that each individual must eventually face for himself. Which way shall I take in regard to this Old Story of Salvation? And why? How will my decision affect my worshiping, praying, singing, and reading, my relations with friends, neighbors, community, and church, and my day-by-day facing of life's opportunities and tragedies?

It will be easier to abandon the effort to change and to conform to popular patterns, to be content with the emotional glow of old symbols even though their old meanings may be gone. There is inevitably something crude about the ways of pioneers in any area of life. It will probably take many years for any group of innovators to create and develop new rituals, new art, new music and drama, new prayers and psalms equal in their beauty and appeal to the old art forms in our Jewish-Christian heritage. And before these new art forms can be created, new ideas must be thought out.

Our generation has seized the fire. Now we must learn to use it and work out our own salvation. We need the glowing spirit of a Prometheus or of a Messiah, not in one person only, but burning in millions of hearts, to rouse us to an unquenchable zest in a co-operative struggle. As long as we fight one another—"the good" against "the bad"—instead of studying to understand one another; as long as we condemn and cast out, rather than draw the larger circle that includes all people and all kinds, our "hope for the world" will turn to dust and ashes.

Yes, some of us believe a greater story is in the making if we and the generations that follow us have the eyes to see it and the ears to hear it, and the persistence in love that is required to make it.

Bibliography and References

1. Philip Schaff, ed., St. Augustine, "The Catechising of the Uninstructed," *The Nicene and Post-Nicene Fathers,* First Series, vol. 3, chap. 2 (New York: Scribner's, 1905), pp. 302-310.

2. One of the Apocryphal books of the Bible, no longer usually included in the Protestant Bible, yet still included in the Catholic Bible.

3. Harold H. Watts, *The Modern Reader's Guide to the Bible* (New York: Harper, 1949).

4. Edgar J. Goodspeed, *The Story of the Bible* (Chicago: University of Chicago Press, 1936).

5. Sophia L. Fahs, *Beginnings of Earth and Sky* (Boston: Beacon Press, 1937). Sophia L. Fahs and Dorothy T. Spoerl, *Beginnings of Life and Death* (Boston: Beacon Press, 1938).

6. Andrew D. White, *A History of the Warfare of Science with Theology in Christendom,* vol. 1 (New York: Appleton, 1896), p. 9.

7. Paul Tillich, "The Meaning and Source of Courage," *Child Study,* Summer, 1954.

8. Robert J. McCracken, sermon preached at Riverside Church, New York City, May 30, 1954.

9. Sigmund Freud, *An Outline of Psychoanalysis,* James Starchy, translator (New York: Norton, 1949).

10. Karen Horney, *Our Inner Conflicts: A Constructive Theory of Neurosis* (New York: Norton, 1945), Introduction and Part I.

11. C. A. and M. M. Aldrich, *Babies Are Human Beings* (New York: Macmillan, 1937). Sophia L. Fahs, *Today's Children and Yesterday's Heritage* (Boston: Beacon Press, 1952), chap. 3. Margaret A. Ribble, *The Rights of Infants: Early Psychological Needs and Their Satisfaction* (New York: Columbia University Press, 1947).

12. Reginald D. Manwell and Sophia L. Fahs, *The Church Across the Street* (Boston: Beacon Press, 1946), chap. 11.

13. Oscar Wilde, *De Profundis* (London: Methuen, 1922).

14. Illustrated card, published by Solace Art Company, New York.

15. Fahs and Spoerl, *op. cit.,* Part II, "Why Do We Die?"

16. Floyd H. Ross and Tynette W. Hills, *Questions That Matter Most: Asked by the World's Religions* (Boston: Beacon Press, 1954).

17. Sophia L. Fahs, *From Long Ago and Many Lands* (Boston: Beacon Press, 1948).

18. John Bigelow, ed., *The Autobiography of Benjamin Franklin* (New York: Putnam, 1909).

19. Lecomte du Nouy, *Human Destiny* (New York: Longmans, Green, 1947).

20. Sir Arthur Keith, "Science Demands Evidence," *New York Times Magazine,* July 8, 1928.

21. Benjamin Jowett, translator, *Phaedo* (dialogue on soul and immortality), *Dialogues of Plato* (New York: Oxford University Press, 1931).

22. Margaret D. Edwards, *Child of the Sun: A Pharaoh of Egypt* (Boston: Beacon Press, 1939).

23. From diary records of sessions of the Church School of Riverside Church, New York City, taught by Lucy Eisenhart and Elizabeth Fleming.

24. Leroy Waterman, *The Religion of Jesus: Christianity's Heritage of Prophetic Religion* (New York: Harper, 1952), p. 103.

25. Isaac Watts.

26. Waterman, *op. cit.,* p. 72.

27. *Ibid.,* p. 157.

28. *Eusebius' Ecclesiastical History,* vol. 3, p. 29.

29. Henry B. Sharman, ed., *The Records of the Life of Jesus* (New York: Association Press, 1917).

30. A. J. Edmunds, translator, *Dhamapada* (Chicago: Open Court, 1902), p. 165.

31. William E. Hocking, *Living Religions and a World Faith* (New York: Macmillan, 1940), pp. 141, 142.

32. Swami Prabhavananda and Christopher Isherwood, translators, *The Song of God: Bhagavad-Gita* (New York: New American Library, 1954), p. 133.

33. Taken from diary records of sessions of the Church School of Riverside Church, New York City, Dr. William Shimer, leader.

34. White, *op. cit.,* vol. 1, p. 25.

35. Ralph Waldo Emerson, Essay on *Circles, Essays,* First Series (New York: John B. Alden, 1890), p. 209.

36. *Idem.*

37. John Bunyan, *The Pilgrim's Progress* (reprint of original made by Century, 1900, and by Thomas Nelson, 1902).

38. A few sample volumes, beautifully illustrated, are:
Albert Bailey, *Christ and His Gospel in Recent Art* (New York: Scribner's, 1948).
Albert Bailey, *The Gospel in Art* (Boston: Pilgrim Press, 1916).
Ira S. Dodd, *The Pictorial Life of Christ* (New York: Christian Herald Press, 1912).
Helen S. Estabrook, compiler, *Old Testament Stories in Woodcut* (Boston: Beacon Press, 1938).
Eliot Hodgkin, *A Pictorial Gospel* (New York: Macmillan, 1950).
John La Farge, *The Gospel Story in Art* (New York: Macmillan, 1950).
Susan N. Pulsifer, compiler, *Scenes from the Life of Jesus in Woodcut* (Boston: Beacon Press, 1947).

39. Alice Cobb, *War's Unconquered Children Speak* (Boston: Beacon Press, 1953).

40. White, *op. cit.,* vol. 1, p. 53.

41. *Christ the Hope of the World,* Document on the Main Theme of the Second Assembly of the World Council of Churches (New York: World Council of Churches, 1954).

42. James H. Nichols, *Evanston: An Interpretation* (New York: Harper, 1954).

43. Bernhard W. Anderson, *Rediscovering the Bible* (New York: Association Press, 1951).

44. Alan W. Watts, *Myth and Ritual in Christianity* (New York: Vanguard Press, 1954).

45. Carleton S. Coon, *The Story of Man: From the first Human Being to Primitive Culture and Beyond* (New York: Alfred Knopf, 1954).
Fritz Kahn, *Design of the Universe: The Heavens and the Earth* (New York: Crown, 1954).
Weston La Barre, *The Human Animal* (Chicago: University of Chicago Press, 1954).
In these three volumes, the authors — two anthropologists and a physicist — attempt to sketch man's entire history, each one adding his own prophesies regarding his potential future.